Contents

C000233355

Running
the race

Do you think of your life as a Christian as a battle? For the apostle Paul, life was a 'fight' and a 'race' (2 Timothy 4:7). What was he fighting against? Spiritual forces of evil, a world wanting to pull him away from God, and his own misdirected desires (Ephesians 2:1–3) – a lot, then! Do we have it any easier? And yet, how important to you is time with God each day? Many readers of *Daily Bread* have faithfully completed each reading each day for years; others can't quite find the discipline. But we all face the same danger of living as if we're in peace time. The reality is there's a war going on – in the world, in the heavens, and in our hearts. So let's not read regularly just out of habit, or read rarely out of busyness – let's read to run the race to win the prize of knowing Jesus, both today and in eternity (2 Timothy 4:8)!

This quarter's readings will help you fight and race. When faced with isolation, Philippians teaches us to maintain a deep connection with God and others; and 2 Timothy and Titus encourage us to pray for our Christian communities and their leaders. 1 Kings 1–10 reminds us of God's sovereignty in keeping his promises to his people. In Matthew 23–25, Jesus asks if, on the Day of Judgement, he will find us ready because our hope is in him. The reality of that Day and seriousness about sin is a great theme of Jeremiah. Keeping God central to life and worship is the challenge of 2 Chronicles. And at the end of the year, we have an opportunity to review what really matters through Ecclesiastes, and refocus on the grace of God at Christmas (Luke 1,2).

In these closing months of the year, let's fight the good fight, and run the race.

Angus Moyes

Editor

How to use *Daily Bread*

Way in

This page introduces both the notes and the writer. It sets the scene and tells you what you need to know to get into each series.

A day's note

The notes for each day include five key elements: Prepare, Read (the Bible passage for the day), Explore, Respond and Bible in a year. These are intended to provide a helpful way of meeting God in his Word.

Prepare yourself to meet with God and pray that the Holy Spirit will help you to understand and respond to what you read.

Read the Bible passage, taking time to absorb and simply enjoy it. A verse or two from the Bible text is usually included on each page, but it's important to read the whole passage.

Explore the meaning of the passage, listening for what God may be saying to you. Before you read the comment, ask yourself: what's the main point of this passage? What is God showing me about himself or about my life? Is there a promise or a command, a warning or example to take special notice of?

Respond to what God has shown you in the passage in worship and pray for yourself and others. Decide how to share your discoveries with others.

Bible in a year If your aim is to know God and his Word more deeply, why not follow this plan to read the whole Bible in one year?

How do we SHINE for God in schools?

Schools are at the centre of our communities. Ask anyone what they think of school and they will be able to tell you, because we've all been there! They are places of education, formation and opportunity. We each made our mark where we went to school, and we have all been impacted. They helped form us into the person we are today.

Schools should help development of the whole person: physical, emotional, mental, social and of course spiritual. Pupils are there five days a week for up to 14 years. This is their 'everyday' space. So how can we help young people live for God at school? After grappling with this question, SHINE was born.

In 2009 Scripture Union NI (suni.co.uk) and Crown Jesus Ministries (crownjesus.org) in Northern Ireland partnered to produce a resource to answer this question.

Nine years later, after a lot of planning, producing and praying, we have grown to include Logos Ministries International (lmi-org.net) and Scripture Union England and Wales (scriptureunion.org.uk) as fellow partners. It has been an incredible journey.

Geoff Brown, Development Worker for SU England and Wales, explains what first excited him about SHINE. 'We had been discussing for a while how we can best support Christian young people to live for God at school. When we heard about SHINE, we thought that it could be a really useful way of doing this without reinventing the wheel.'

Encouraged by new partnerships, the purpose remains the same:

• To EQUIP young people to live for God in school.

• To allow young people to EXPLORE the Bible and Jesus for themselves.

• To encourage young people to PRAY for their schools.

The premise is to get groups across the UK doing this at the same time of the year. There is something powerful when we show partnership in the gospel and see the bigger picture of what God is doing (and the picture certainly got bigger when SU England and Wales came on board!).

Aiming for the month of November (or if that isn't possible, they are free to participate at another time during the school year), we ask groups to take three weeks to run SHINE. During the first two weeks the groups show videos that we have produced, with the third week as an event week. Every year there is a different theme – 'Do Something', 'Roadtrip: The Journey' being some recent examples. The videos are tailored to meet the needs of the individual group as every context is different and unique. They vary in length depending on whether a school group meets at lunch time or after school, and in content depending on the set-up of the group.

In the third week, the SHINE event week challenges pupils to invite their friends along to the Christian group. Again, every school is different in what they do. Some run an 'ice cream factory' and share the gospel. Others do 'Tea, Toast and Testimonies' as pupils have the courage and boldness to stand up and share how God has been working in their lives. Some book their assembly hall and bring a special guest in to perform a particular skill or talent before sharing about Jesus.

The reason we believe the project works so well is because it can be tailor-made for any setting. It gives Christian groups in schools a focus and resources with enough flexibility to make it their own. We try to make it as easy a process as possible, providing all material through our website.

After seeing this model work with young people, we are excited to say that it is being rolled out in primary schools too. The purpose will remain the same, but the timing needs to be different, with February most likely. We are really excited about the potential of 'SHINE kids' and expectant to hear all the stories of God working through it.

For us, it is a real joy to be able to partner for the gospel and produce a resource to help so many Christian groups in schools. We're thankful for all the feedback we've received about the impact the videos and events have been having. Here are some examples from group leaders involved in SHINE 2017:

'A group of Year 12 boys (some unlikely lads) came to our doughnut challenge on the third week. Our numbers doubled that week and some returned the next week.'

'To see the pupil committee who organised the whole event in such an earnest manner pull together and put so much energy and effort into it was wonderful.'

It's been great to see how pupils have taken up the opportunity to live for God in their schools, to hear about non-Christians invited along to a Christian group, and testimonies being shared for the first time. Many have had the chance to explore Christianity for themselves as Christian young people pray for their friends and their school.

For more information on SHINE or SHINE kids, head to the websites:
www.shineinschools.com
www.shinekids.co.uk

Phil Howe

Post-primary schools coordinator, SU Northern Ireland

Scripture Union presents...

Scripture Union

A new format for

light

Bubbles – Under 5s
£34.99

Splash! – 5 to 8s
£34.99

Xstream – 8 to 11s
£34.99

theGRID – 11 to 14s
£34.99

Our bestselling Light curriculum is going annual.

- 52 Bible-based sessions • Ready-to-use options
- All resources photocopiable • Everything you need to run each session

Make it real

Writer

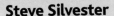

Steve Silvester

Steve leads St Nic's, Nottingham, a city-centre church dedicated to growing disciples of Jesus. He also leads 'City Prayer', a movement uniting churches across the city.

One of the most challenging questions I have had to contemplate is this: 'Is my life worthy of imitation?' Paul had no trouble encouraging the church at Philippi to follow his example. Indeed he saw his life as a model for others to replicate (Philippians 3:17). Last week's readings concluded with the great hymn about the life of Jesus (2:6–11). What does that life look like in you and me? As someone else put it, I am called to live the life that Jesus would live if he were me.

The rest of this letter covers territory that we are all familiar with in our daily lives: living in a warped society; struggling to be generous with our friendships; navigating the 'narrow way' without falling into legalism or careless living; working through disagreements; keeping our attitudes right; learning to depend on God's provision. How can we possibly 'live the life'?

As we read the New Testament it becomes clear that this life has actually been planted in every Christian. It will flourish all by itself just as a plant does if it receives adequate sunlight and water, and if its soil is not invaded by competing plants. Paul writes elsewhere, 'We always carry around in our body the death of Jesus, *so that the life* of Jesus may also be *revealed* in our body' (2 Corinthians 4:10, italics added).

These later chapters of Paul's letter can help us to discover more about living 'the life' which is distinctive in any generation and which, ultimately, is the life of Jesus.

The outworking

Prepare

How does your life measure up to what you believe? Ask the Lord to show you. Give thanks for his work in your life.

Read   Philippians 2:12–18

Explore

The final service of a wonderful Christian festival had just come to an end. Worship songs were still ringing in our ears as we climbed into our vehicles to head home. But while we were singing there had been a terrible storm. The car park was a mud bath and cars were veering all over the place. Tempers quickly became frayed in the dash to the exit. It was time for our worship to be outworked in our driving!

Caught up in the great hymn to Jesus (vs 6–11) the Philippians may have forgotten that Paul has just asked them to do something (vs 2,3). The hymn exalted Jesus' obedience, 'even to the point of death'. Would they now be obedient? Israel had been a 'warped and crooked generation' (Deuteronomy 32:5), a phrase applied to contemporary society in Philippi. Israel had grumbled and questioned Moses' leadership (Exodus 16:7; Numbers 11:1). By contrast, the Philippian church is to shine with the beauty and obedience of Christ (v 15b). For them it meant outworking their salvation in their relationships; for Paul it might mean a martyr's death (v 17). Either way, they were not alone: the outworking of our faith, and even the desire to do so, is the work of God (v 13).

> *Therefore, my dear friends, as you have always obeyed – not only in my presence, but now much more in my absence – continue to work out your salvation with fear and trembling …*
>
> Philippians 2:12 (NIV)

Respond

Despite his circumstances, Paul is full of joy (v 17). Obedience is the path to joy. Choose joy!

Bible in a Year
Isaiah 61,62; Hebrews 12

9

Philippians 2:19–30

HR briefing

> So then, welcome him in the Lord with great joy, and honour people like him …
>
> Philippians 2:29 (NIV)

Prepare

Jesus sent his disciples on mission in pairs (Luke 9,10). It is important to know who our partners are, to value them and speak well of them. Who is in your 'team'?

Read   Philippians 2:19–30

Explore

Paul did not have a large infrastructure to support his ministry. The churches he founded did not have an established culture of supporting their apostle financially (see 4:15). His travelling team was small and tight-knit. To lose one of these men would be a blow. Here, at a time of great personal need, Paul contemplates losing *two* for the sake of the Philippian church.

Timothy is Paul's preferred choice. Timothy is like a son to Paul, working alongside him and best placed to represent the apostle (vs 22,20). But his departure must be delayed until Paul's future is more clear (v 23). So the immediate envoy will be Epaphroditus, recently recovered from a life-threatening illness, who has been alongside Paul through thick and thin.

Paul has warned of the destructive dangers of self-interest (2:4). In his desperate circumstances of imprisonment and uncertainty about the future, he has seen self-interest affect people very close to him (v 21). His selfless decision to send his closest colleagues powerfully embodied the 'mind of Christ' he was urging the Philippian church to have.

Respond

Great teams, like Paul's, have a purpose that is bigger than itself. A family, a married couple, a group of friends, can all be great teams. Pray for your 'team' to be free of self-interest and totally committed to the cause of Christ.

Bible in a Year
Isaiah 63,64; Hebrews 13

The real deal

Prepare

You may be familiar with the idea of a SWOT analysis. Thinking of your situation, where do you see Strengths, Weaknesses, Opportunities and Threats?

Read   Philippians 3:1–11

Explore

The first word of verse 1 ('finally' or 'further') could be either completing the previous line of thought or beginning a new one. Either way, this section of the letter does take a sudden change of direction with the encouragement to rejoice being resumed at 4:4. It is as though Paul is suddenly seized by concern for the church at Philippi. It is in danger of being infiltrated by 'Judaisers' insisting that non-Jewish converts to Christianity should become Jews first, and therefore be circumcised.

Paul is all too familiar with this thinking. It constantly aspires to greater perfection according to a clearly defined scale of religious qualifications. Paul himself has been at the very top of this scale (vs 5,6). But he has come to see that what he considered 'strengths' were actually weaknesses, and what he considered 'threats' were in fact opportunities (v 7; see 2 Corinthians 12:1–10). Only one thing matters: knowing Christ and having the righteousness that comes from faith in him, not through religious 'achievements'.

> *What is more, I consider everything a loss because of the surpassing worth of knowing Christ Jesus my Lord, for whose sake I have lost all things. I consider them garbage, that I may gain Christ …*
> **Philippians 3:8 (NIV)**

Respond

Are my spiritual aspirations really centred on 'knowing Christ'? Could his way involve things I have considered losses or threats (including suffering, v 10)?

Philippians 3:12–21

The finishing line

> *I press on towards the goal to win the prize for which God has called me heavenwards in Christ Jesus.*
>
> Philippians 3:14 (NIV)

Prepare

'Christ Jesus has made me his own' (Philippians 3:12, NRSV). Spend some time meditating on this statement.

Read   Philippians 3:12–21

Explore

I once delivered a sermon on a bicycle, pedaling around the church. I was trying to illustrate the fact that much of Paul's writing is combating two extremes. Just as it is possible to fall off a bicycle to the left or the right, Paul argues that it is possible to misunderstand the Christian gospel by leaning too hard either towards 'duty' (*it all depends on you*) or towards 'freedom' (*Christ has set us free from the law, so do as you like*). He has just been warning against legalism. But there were also 'enemies of the cross' (v 18) who used the resurrection victory of Jesus as a pretext to indulge their every desire (v 19). Following either set of false teachers would lead to a painful crash.

So Paul offers the church a way forward: 'join together in following my example' (v 17a). They have observed Paul 'riding without stabilisers', sometimes seeming to lean one way, sometimes the other, but always looking forward (vs 13,20), not crashing. Others have mastered this art too (v 17b). The secret to this wonderful balance lies in verse 12: '*I press on to make [the prize] my own because Christ Jesus* has made me his own' (NRSV). As Christ holds me in his hands, I am to reach out my hands to take hold of the prize.

Respond

What is your tendency: towards 'duty' or towards 'freedom'? What is the best way to guard against this danger?

12

Philippians 4:1–9

One mind

Prepare

Make a list of the things that currently cause you anxiety and concern, especially any relationships that are stressful. Over each item read the key verse (Philippians 4:5).

Read   Philippians 4:1–9

Explore

Paul arrives at the most sensitive part of his letter, where he names the women at the heart of a problem in the Philippian church, Euodia and Syntyche. Were they among Lydia's friends who first heard the gospel from Paul (Acts 16:13)? We don't know. They had 'struggled alongside' Paul in ministry but now their disagreement was having a damaging effect on the church. Sadly, it is often those who have invested so much of themselves in Christ's work who find it hardest to lay down differences.

Paul reminds them that they are defined not by difference but by what they share. In an obvious reference back to 2:5 he urges them to be 'of the same mind'. In our age of individualism, which encourages us to emphasise our uniqueness, we easily forget that maturity in Christ makes us alike (3:15) as it makes us like Christ.

Euodia and Syntyche may not arrive at the same views on particular issues; but they can arrive at one mind. The mind of Christ is one of humility and trust in God. God's presence with them (v 5b), and a focus on the right things (v 8) should help them keep their disagreements in perspective.

> *Let your gentleness be evident to all. The Lord is near.*
> Philippians 4:5 (NIV)

Respond

Are you in disagreement with anyone? Is this damaging others? Use this passage to help you discern what is important. In particular, examine your attitudes in the light of these verses.

Bible in a Year
Jeremiah 3,4; John 2

Saturday
6 October

Gratitude, the source of joy

> And my God will meet all your needs according to the riches of his glory in Christ Jesus.
>
> Philippians 4:19 (NIV)

Prepare

Spend some time giving thanks to God, especially for the relationships through which you experience his love and care.

Read   Philippians 4:10–23

Explore

When this letter was read out to the church in Philippi it would have been easy for the hearers to forget that Paul was actually in a far more challenging situation than themselves. Throughout the letter there are outbursts of joy, especially in this final chapter (4:1,4,10).

Paul knows that he needs to put his trust in God. People can be unreliable (2:21), but God can be trusted in all circumstances (v 12). Verse 13 is often taken as an expression of self-sufficiency: I have God, so I don't need anyone else. However, this is not a biblical position. It is not good for human beings to be alone (Genesis 2:18). The practical support of the Philippian church means a great deal to Paul (vs 10,14). God does indeed meet all his needs, but his method of doing so is often through other people.

The relationship between Paul and this church is a practical outworking of this truth: Jesus' birth, death and resurrection have united God and humanity (2:5–11); all who are 'in Christ' are also profoundly connected to one another; the life of Christ is at work in them (1:21) and they share the mind of Christ (2:5; 4:2). It is all God's work and he alone deserves the praise (v 20).

Respond

Are there any relationships that you should value more because they are God's gift to you? Are there relationships of which your expectations are unrealistic and a substitute for God?

Bible in a Year
Jeremiah 5,6; John 3

Strong in the Lord

Prepare

'Be strong in the Lord and in his mighty power'
(Ephesians 6:10). Think of some of the challenges
you face. Find your strength in the Lord.

Read   Psalm 20

Explore

This is a psalm 'of', 'for' or 'concerning' David. It
probably had a ceremonial use in the life of Israel
as the nation prayed for its king. We could imagine
verses 1 to 5 being said or sung by the priests and
people, verses 6 to 8 by the king, with the final
verse being the resounding response of the priests
and people.

Every nation wants its leader to be strong,
but expectations can be burdensome. Any king
for whom this psalm is used could not fail to be
confident, strong and hopeful. The day of 'distress'
(v 1) becomes a day of opportunity because
ultimately the people are not looking to their king
but to God. The king would know that his people
are behind him and that God is for him. Like Joshua
before him he could 'be strong and courageous'
(Joshua 1:9).

This psalm is a prayer, but it is also an act of
blessing. How much stronger would our leaders,
children, spouses, friends and colleagues be if we
learned to speak blessing over them? David was
a great leader. He lived out of the strength that
comes from blessing (see 2 Samuel 23:1). Similarly,
Jesus ministered from the confidence that he
derived from his Father's blessing (Mark 1:11).

*Some trust in chariots
and some in horses, but
we trust in the name of
the Lord our God.*
Psalm 20:7 (NIV)

Respond

What strength can you
derive from the blessings
of this psalm? Which
words and phrases could
you use to pray for, and to
bless, others?

Bible in a Year
Jeremiah 7,8; Psalms 114,115

Blessed: wisdom and wealth

Writer

Mark Meynell

Mark is a husband, father and pastor – passionate about building bridges between cultures, and between the ancient Scriptures and contemporary world.

An absolute monarch's business of leading a kingdom must be as far removed from the lifestyles of most *Daily Bread* readers as it is possible to be! But the period during which King Solomon consolidated his authority over Israel is no mere historical curiosity. We learn a great deal about the realities of human power, for good or ill. But we learn even more about the God who created the nation of Israel from scratch, and then raised up leaders to keep them faithful to him. He is a promise-making and promise-keeping God. That truth is the thread that ties the whole of Old Testament history together.

But no reader of 1 Kings can overlook some of the more disturbing aspects of these events. Throughout Israel's history, people have had feet of clay. In our chapters, Solomon fares well on the whole – the darker aspects of his reign come from 1 Kings 11. But he is not perfect.

This is why the Christian reader will always be looking forward to the time when the best will come. Every Old Testament king was anointed for the role. As such, each is technically *'messiah'* (or *'Christ'* in Greek). 'Christ' Solomon had his good points but also his deep flaws – despite nobly seeking wisdom from God when given the choice of anything he wanted.

We can rejoice that the perfect king, Christ Jesus, has come. Anything that is good in Solomon is perfected in Jesus.

1 Kings 1:1–27

Fragile kingdom

Prepare

Ancient court politics probably feels far removed from your day. But we have all experienced fearing for the future when the present is full of uncertainty. This was Israel's predicament as David's reign drew to its close.

Read   1 Kings 1:1–27

Explore

Whenever the sultan of the old Ottoman Empire died, his sons would hurtle to Istanbul. The first one back would seize the crown and invariably have his rival brothers executed. That was something of the situation in Jerusalem. David had many sons and it was clear that his days were numbered. Nobody could fail to spot the contrast between David's feeble frailty (vs 1–4) and the vigorous but headstrong Adonijah (vs 5,6). Immediately the court divides into pro- and anti-Adonijah factions (vs 7–9).

Adonijah's ambitions are only thwarted by Nathan's quick thinking and political savvy (vs 10–17). Nathan then goes to David himself to back up Bathsheba (vs 18–27). The key issue is that David has pledged that Solomon would succeed him – note that the phrase 'surely Solomon your son shall be king after me' (v 13) is alluded to eight more times in this chapter. Disastrously, David never did anything official about that (just as he failed to challenge Adonijah's behaviour, v 6). Perhaps due to his age, he neglected his responsibilities as king and father. What a desperate end to a remarkable life.

> *Go in to King David and say to him, 'My lord the king, did you not swear to me your servant: "Surely Solomon your son shall be king after me, and he will sit on my throne"? Why then has Adonijah become king?'*
>
> 1 Kings 1:13 (NIV)

Respond

What do you do when God's work seems to totter? If God in Christ is really sovereign and ruler, we surely do two things: pray for the protection of his kingdom; pray for the wisdom of those with responsibilities to lead (especially if that includes you!).

Tuesday
9 October

1 Kings 1:28–53

David wakes in time

> 'As the Lᴏʀᴅ was with my lord the king, so may he be with Solomon to make his throne even greater than the throne of my lord King David!'
>
> 1 Kings 1:37 (NIV)

Prepare

Facing reality can be hard, but wishful thinking cannot change facts. Just as all must accept the laws of gravity (however much they would like to fly), so we must acknowledge God's chosen king.

Read   1 Kings 1:28–53

Explore

Nathan's speedy appraisal of Israel's dicey situation pays off. In the nick of time, he has spurred the aged David to wake up to what was really happening around him. Once again, he suddenly looks like the true king he had been. What a relief it must have been for those who cared about the welfare of God's Israel!

His succession plans are more than just an idle wish. He had sworn on oath to God that it would happen (vs 29,30). This makes his failure to make a clear proclamation to the nation about this all the stranger. Is there a trace of irony in Bathsheba's courtly response (v 31)? After all, the whole point is to clarify his successor! Even if there is, though, she does speak truth, for the gospel of great David's greater Son – Jesus – promises exactly that.

Everything then happens quickly (vs 32–40). On David's orders, Zadok anoints Solomon king, and there is now nothing Adonijah can do about it. He must face reality – and realises that he is entirely at Solomon's mercy (vs 50,51). The new king shows his brother magnanimous grace – to begin with (vs 52,53)…

Respond

Sin's essence is the desire to seize from God's rightful rule the throne over our own and others' lives. Pray for forgiveness for the spirit of Adonijah and a willingness to bow the knee to King Jesus.

Bible in a Year
Jeremiah 11,12; John 5

1 Kings 2:1–12

Parting priorities

Prepare

Royal Jerusalem was dangerous. The threat of palace coups and breakaway factions was constant. But leadership brings dilemmas. And just because God's people advocate certain courses of action, we shouldn't assume they always get it right.

> *So Solomon sat on the throne of his father David, and his rule was firmly established.*
> 1 Kings 2:12 (NIV)

Read

1 Kings 2:1–12

Explore

David gives Solomon two priorities (vs 1–4). This is not standard political fare, is it?! It would be unthinkable to hear politicians today suggest that a leader's first priority is their relationship with God. Yet this is precisely what matters to David – Solomon is *God's* king. The instructions are little different from those for all Old Covenant believers (blessings for faithfulness, Deuteronomy 28:1,2, or curses for unfaithfulness, Deuteronomy 28:15). The difference is Solomon's responsibility to take the lead in faithfulness. As Israel's history would repeatedly prove, a king's unfaithfulness had a devastating effect on the whole nation.

In total contrast, David's second priority seems entirely predictable in worldly politics… tragically (see vs 5–12). But it seems horribly out of place for God's king. This is where Old Testament foreshadowing of the great King begins to seem very blurry (as the rest of chapter 2 illustrates). There is a principle at work, though – the protection and solidifying of the king's rule. It requires great wisdom (v 9) and strong measures. It is never wise to challenge God's purposes.

Respond

God will deal with the threats to the rule of his Christ. But praise God that in Jesus Christ, we find the greatest King who dies for his enemies, even forgiving the soldiers who crucified him.

1 Kings 3:1–15

God-given wisdom

> 'So give your servant a discerning heart to govern your people and to distinguish between right and wrong. For who is able to govern this great people of yours?'
>
> 1 Kings 3:9 (NIV)

Prepare

We're not monarchs, palace courtiers, or Old Covenant priests or prophets. But this does not make 1 Kings irrelevant. Because we *are* called to trust in the same God. Consider what you depend on him for the most.

Read   1 Kings 3:1–15

Explore

As so often with Old Testament history, we are just given the bald facts with little comment – inviting us to draw our own conclusions from the rest of Scripture. In the light of what is to come later in 1 and 2 Kings, two details stand out like flashing red lights: first, Solomon marries Pharaoh's daughter (3:1)! This is going to have serious repercussions (see 11:1–6). Second, people were still sacrificing on the high places – there was no alternative (v 2). This is what brings the king to Gibeon (v 4). But once the Temple is built, these will be a great snare, even for the king (see 11:7; 12:31,32). Despite this, what is clear about the king's spiritual state (v 3)?

Given his unique God-given opportunity (v 5), Solomon makes the most remarkable request. Note how he sees everything in the light of what God has already done for David and Israel (v 6). Why is that important? Verses 7 to 9 show that Solomon has taken his father's instructions (from yesterday's passage) to heart. What better gift could there be?

The Lord is more than generous in his response (vs 10–14). The following chapters prove that God keeps his promises.

Respond

James 1:5 reminds us *all* to seek God's wisdom. Spend some time in prayer, seeking forgiveness for falling short and praying for wisdom.

Bible in a Year
Jeremiah 15,16; Psalm 116

Wisdom's acid test

Friday
12 October

Prepare

Jesus told us to be as wise as serpents but as innocent as doves (Matthew 10:16). Bring to him any areas of life that require such wisdom.

Read   1 Kings 3:16–28

Explore

One person's word against another's (vs 22,23). It's the classic but painful dilemma of relationship breakdown. In this case, it's made even more tragic by the terrible loss of a child. How does one tell truth from lies? Entire professions have grown up over the generations to attempt precisely this.

Now that Israel's monarchy is firmly established, the king has the responsibility to adjudicate in difficult situations (like the judges of old). After listening to these two women's complaints, he is decisive and seemingly brutal. Slice the baby in two (vs 24,25)! What makes this response so shrewd? Above all, it shows deep psychological insight. No doubt the women's reactions were entirely as he predicted (v 26). The one whose child had already died would perhaps have felt a grim satisfaction if both of them ended up grieving. Isn't it astonishing what our self-centredness can justify?

The theme of right judgement is clear throughout: see the recurrence of *'discerning'*, *'distinguish right and wrong'*, *'wisdom'*. Solomon had asked for them (v 9). God provided. The key thing is that justice was done. And it was seen to be done (v 28). But the people were in no doubt about the origins of this wisdom.

> *He then gave an order: 'Cut the living child in two and give half to one and half to the other.'*
> 1 Kings 3:25 (NIV)

Respond

What a relief to know that the final judgement is in safe hands. Solomon's descendant and our King will get it right. Praise him. And pray for others to lean on his mercy before it is too late.

Bible in a Year
Jeremiah 17,18; John 7

1 Kings 4:29–34

Whole life wisdom

From all nations people came to listen to Solomon's wisdom, sent by all the kings of the world, who had heard of his wisdom.

1 Kings 4:34 (NIV)

Prepare

When you pray for others or yourself, do you restrict prayers to 'the religious bits', assuming God is not interested in the mundane details of life?

Read   1 Kings 4:29–34

Explore

After a dry (to us) list of Solomon's key officials (vs 1–19) and Israel's agricultural and military resources (vs 20–28), the writer gives us this thumbnail sketch of the king himself. But these paragraphs do fit together: God is concerned with it *all*.

This can read at first like an example of good old hero-worship, but the point is to show what happens when God's king lives out God's wisdom.

Solomon's reputation for wisdom exceeds all others of the time (vs 29–31) – even if there is some loyal exaggeration here, the important point is that 'his fame spread to all the surrounding nations'. It is the king's wisdom which has brought all the details of verses 1 to 28 together.

He shares the fruits of his wisdom in written and sung form – which only serves to extend his reputation still further (v 32). Many of these, of course, ended up in the book of Proverbs.

Unexpectedly, divine wisdom even embraces natural history (v 33). But that stands to reason if God has made everything, and wisdom is a matter of living in *his* world *his* way. There is nothing in all the world that is beyond God's interest or concern.

Respond

Pray through each commitment you have in the coming week, regardless of whether it is church-related or not. Pray for God's wisdom so that each can serve his kingdom.

Bible in a Year
Jeremiah 19,20; John 8

Psalm 21:1–13

Sunday
14 October

The King's heart's desire

Prepare

Count your blessings: it's a vital spiritual discipline!

Read   Psalm 21:1–13

Explore

This is the perfect psalm to read soon after Solomon's request for wisdom, since his father reflects on all that God has given him. Identify the different ways that God has shown his blessing to his anointed king in these verses.

There is always a danger that one's heart's desires are merely a reflection of selfish ambitions or sinful passions. When God grants his king whatever he desires, we can be sure that he would never indulge them. The crucial point is the fact that David has his relationship with God on the right track. He trusts him (v 7)!

The heart of his confidence in God lies with that wonderful Hebrew word translated in the NIV as *unfailing love*. It is almost impossible to translate into any language. But it includes God's faithfulness to his covenant promises, his kindness and gentleness, his love and purpose for us to flourish. All of this is *promised*. That is the grounds of confidence. God's rule must be upheld (vs 8–13). We will never understand his judgement if we assume it is anything like human short-temperedness or rage. It is fundamentally different – it is his settled hostility to sin. A universe where he did nothing about evil and injustice would be terrifying. This is the reason for praise and gratitude to God for his justice (v 13 – compare with Revelation 19:1,2).

You have granted him his heart's desire and have not withheld the request of his lips.
Psalm 21:2 (NIV)

Respond

Give thanks that through Jesus, every one of us can relish God's love. Reflect on how that gives us confidence to persevere with him.

Bible in a Year
Jeremiah 21,22; Psalms 117,118

23

1 Kings 5:1–18

A promised duty

> The LORD gave Solomon wisdom, just as he had promised him. There were peaceful relations between Hiram and Solomon, and the two of them made a treaty.
>
> 1 Kings 5:12 (NIV)

Prepare

Reflect on this: true rest is still to come.

Read
1 Kings 5:1–18

Explore

Today's passage needs a bit of background to make most sense. King David had rest from his enemies and realised he lived in a palace while God 'lived' in a tent. So he offered to build a temple (2 Samuel 7:1,2). God responded with promises: 1) Present peace is only a foretaste of the heavenly rest to be brought by God's eternal King (2 Samuel 7:10). 2) God will provide David with a house (dynasty), not the other way around (2 Samuel 7:11,12). 3) God promises David's descendant will build a physical house (2 Samuel 7:13).

In our present passage, Solomon takes advantage of diplomatic moves from King Hiram of Tyre, and arranges a treaty with the region famed for its remarkable cedar trees (vs 1–6). Even more remarkable is Hiram's delighted response. He praises the God of Israel, for David's successor (v 7). Here is a Gentile king acknowledging the divinely granted wisdom of Israel's king.

The building of this house for God put great burdens on the nation in payment (v 11) and manpower (vs 13–18). But it was worth it! An established Temple, which would be the focal point for the whole nation's commitment to their Creator God, would do away with the allure for the 'high places' at a stroke.

Respond

We do not meet God in a Temple any longer (Jesus *is* our Temple – see John 2:21,22). Yet the privilege of meeting God is still extremely costly. But Christ paid the price by dying. Rejoice in this great privilege!

Bible in a Year
Jeremiah 23,24; John 9

Promised resting place

Prepare

How well do you cope with waiting? Especially without any foreseeable let-up? Most of us struggle with that, I suspect. But what if God has promised something? How do you keep going while you wait?

Read   1 Kings 8:1–21

Explore

Israel had had a long wait. So the completion and dedication of the Temple did not simply call for a celebration of an architectural job well done. This marked a national turning point, a symbol of centuries of wandering drawing to a close.

From the Exodus from Egypt onwards, the Ark of the Covenant (v 9) had been kept in a special tent. But now it could be brought out of the tent (v 4) and into the Most Holy Place in the new building. This marked true confidence in their God-given rest from their enemies (as promised in 2 Samuel 7) because the whole point of the Temple is that it is *not* portable! No wonder all the great and the good attend this moment (vs 1,2). This is the culmination of centuries of hope!

With great care and ceremony, the priests take the Ark to its final resting place (vs 6–9; see 2 Samuel 6:7). The climax comes when the cloud descends – just as it had nearly a millennium before during the wilderness wanderings (vs 10–12). What confidence it brings to know that God is living with his people. No wonder Solomon bursts into praise (vs 14–21). But notice the theme: God's promises *kept*!

> *'The Lord has kept the promise he made: I have succeeded David my father and now I sit on the throne of Israel, just as the Lord promised, and I have built the temple for the Name of the Lord, the God of Israel.'*
>
> 1 Kings 8:20 (NIV)

Respond

Through Jesus, God lives with us, his people. Praise him for the privilege of access to him *without* the need for temples.

1 Kings 8:22–30

Is your God too small?

'But will God really dwell on earth? The heavens, even the highest heaven, cannot contain you. How much less this temple I have built!'

1 Kings 8:27 (NIV)

Prepare

A building, such as a great medieval cathedral, can sometimes lift our spiritual sights to realities beyond our world. Which is ironic because buildings, by definition, set limits on our sight-lines. Has this ever happened to you?

Read   1 Kings 8:22–30

Explore

The Jerusalem Temple did that to an even greater extent – after all, it conformed to divinely revealed plans. Solomon's prayer of dedication is entirely fitting therefore.

Notice how the king begins: Lord – the covenant-making and covenant-keeping God (v 23). He is the God of Israel – a tiny nation occupying a small strip that effectively provides a land bridge between three continents. Yet this God is truly unique.

Work through these verses and identify what sets Israel's God apart from every other object of human worship. The key is surely the fact that no other gods actually reveal promises, let alone keep them. In contrast, Solomon could say that his very position, and the building of the Temple, were the result of promises to his father David.

Casual observers might assume that the Lord was like all the rest simply because he was worshipped in a human building. But Solomon is adamant – God doesn't actually *live* there (vs 27–30). He's far too great for that. Heaven is his home (v 30); the Temple is the visible emblem of his dwelling with his people.

Respond

Spend time reflecting on the fact that God in Christ is revealed as cosmic. The universe is his. Anything we see on earth is just a reflection, a pointer to who he really is.

Bible in a Year
Jeremiah 27,28; John 11

The promise of prayer

Prepare

Why did the Temple exist in the first place? Why was the entire sacrificial system necessary?

Read   1 Kings 8:46–61

Explore

Solomon now identifies the key reasons for visiting the Temple. Each proves that dependence on God lies at its heart (note the six reasons given in verses 31–45). Now comes the seventh and central reason in verse 46. Solomon is not telling God something he doesn't already know. The very existence of the Temple presupposes our sinfulness *and* God's commitment to forgive. Verses 46 to 49 allude to the period of the judges. They didn't have the Temple then, of course, but they did endure this depressing cycle *12 times*!

Israel sins ⇒ Israel handed over to enemies ⇒ Israel repents ⇒ God forgives and restores.

On this basis, the king prays for God to continue the same commitment. Now that the Temple is built, it should be much harder for Israel to forget the covenant. Notice his plea on the basis of what God did in constituting Israel after their rescue from Egypt (vs 50,51). If God did that, why *wouldn't* he forgive them? The Temple is in keeping with God's character – he *longs* to forgive. This is a watershed moment in Israel's history (vs 54–61). A permanent home for the Ark marks the end of their nomadic existence. Solomon blesses the nation – but not just for their own sake. The whole world would be blessed through it (v 60; see Genesis 12:1–3).

> 'May your eyes be open to your servant's plea and to the plea of your people Israel, and may you listen to them whenever they cry out to you.'
> 1 Kings 8:52 (NIV)

Respond

Hebrews shows how Christ's death makes the Temple redundant. Reflect on Hebrews 10:19–22 – confess your sin, but wonder at being cleansed and forgiven.

Bible in a Year
Jeremiah 29–31; Psalm 119:1–24

Friday
19 October

The promised condition

> 'As for you, if you walk before me faithfully with integrity of heart and uprightness, as David your father did, and do all I command and observe my decrees and laws, I will establish your royal throne over Israel for ever, as I promised David your father ...'
>
> 1 Kings 9:4,5a (NIV)

Prepare

Pray that the Lord would impress on you even familiar old truths afresh.

Read   1 Kings 9:1–19

Explore

God appears to Solomon again at Gibeon (see ch 3). Previously, he had praised the king for his request for wisdom. Now he reminds him of what he had repeatedly revealed ever since Moses' day. The Old Covenant is a God-given agreement that requires both parties to keep their sides of the deal. God promises to keep his side: he will be with his people (v 3). But because the nation is represented by King Solomon, their fate lies in his hands. The key word is *if*: if he is faithful... (vs 4,5); if he is unfaithful... (vs 6–9).

None of this is news (glance back at 2:1–12). The difference is that now the primary responsibility lies with the king. God had made that clear to David (in 2 Samuel 7) and David no doubt reminded his son. This is crucial for understanding Israel's subsequent history, right up to the Exile in Babylon. The writer of 1 and 2 Kings keeps reminding us of what God says here, so that the Temple's destruction many years later comes as no surprise.

Now for the realities of rule (vs 10–19). It is not without its challenges or controversies. We baulk at the casual handover of cities, or the use of forced labour. But remember – the writer rarely comments. He merely describes reality. Nevertheless, the nation thrived under Solomon – for now...

Respond

Praise God that we have a King in Jesus who was constantly faithful to God throughout his life, even to the cross.

Bible in a Year
Jeremiah 32,33; John 12

1 Kings 10:1–13,23–25

Saturday
20 October

The promised climax

Prepare

You're climbing a hill. You make steady, if tiring, progress… there's the top! But once there, it's a false summit! The real peak is much higher. This chapter has the same feel.

Read   1 Kings 10:1–13,23–25

Explore

This is the climax of the Old Testament! How far Israel has come from being a family of nomads wandering with their herds. When Genesis ended, they were a family of 70 people descended from Abraham. They had no home, and they hardly constituted a nation. But God had made his promises. Not only would they have both, but they would be a blessing to all nations. Now it has come about: the nation has peace in its borders (see 8:56), the king is secure in his capital, and with the new Temple, the Lord is visibly central to national life.

And now, an African queen arrives. What impresses her most? Who gets the credit for it? How does this relate to Solomon's dream at Gibeon (3:10–14)?

The exchange of glittering gifts and lavish hospitality can distract us from the most amazing aspect of this. A pagan queen praises the Lord in astonishing terms (v 9). She seems clearly to have understood the covenant, because she recognises that it derives from God's everlasting love. These were Israel's glory days – never again to be repeated after Solomon's death.

'Praise be to the LORD your God, who has delighted in you and placed you on the throne of Israel. Because of the LORD's eternal love for Israel, he has made you king to maintain justice and righteousness.'

1 Kings 10:9 (NIV)

Respond

If we know Christ, we have something far greater than Solomon – the truly wise King who has lavished his grace on us. Through him we have eternal treasure. Praise him for that!

Bible in a Year
Jeremiah 34,35; John 13

Sunday
21 October

db

The ultimate sacrifice

> They will proclaim his righteousness, declaring to a people yet unborn: He has done it!
>
> Psalm 22:31 (NIV)

Prepare

Spend a moment in quiet reflection, as before taking the bread and the wine. Come before the Lord in confession for sins in the last week.

Read   Psalm 22

Explore

What different agonies afflict David from the world around him? Why does his faith make things harder for him (vs 1–8)? It is profoundly unsettling that David's first utterance in the psalm is to complain of God's absence. But that is what it *felt* like. What is so hard to figure out is that it seemed to undermine precisely what God has promised.

David describes his suffering in vivid terms: external threats (vs 12,13) and internal pains (vs 14,15). So he prays. His cries plead on the basis of what God has done and who he is (vs 9–11,19–21). The word translated 'LORD' (in capital letters) is the name revealed to Moses at the burning bush (Exodus 3) – he is the promise-making and promise-keeping God.

After the horrors of the previous verses, David's confident hope in this section (vs 22–31) is inspiring. He will declare God's rescue (v 22). Not only will Israel hear of it (v 23) but so will the rest of the world (v 27).

But the most astonishing thing of all is that where David felt forsaken (v 1) but was then rescued, his greatest Son, Jesus, actually *was* forsaken on the cross – but raised that first Easter. It is no accident that he cries out verses 1 *and* 31 from the cross.

Respond

Christ did all this *for you*! Trust that he has done everything needed to bring you full forgiveness and hope for eternity with him.

Bible in a Year
Jeremiah 36,37; Psalm 119:25–48

Be prepared

Writer

Michele Smart

Michele is a writer and editor. She lives on Sydney's northern beaches with her husband, two kids and dog. She surfs badly.

This section of Matthew contains the final teachings of Jesus before he faces his crucifixion. Jesus and his disciples are now in Jerusalem, and Jesus has come into increasing conflict with Jerusalem's religious leaders after entering the city triumphantly on Palm Sunday as Messiah, Israel's King (Matthew 21:1–10). Jesus' disciples are expecting more glory to come – of course the Messiah will kick out the occupying Romans and take power! But in these passages Jesus completely overturns their assumptions.

Jesus' extended discourse here is sobering. At the Temple, he openly condemns the hypocrisy of the Pharisees and Teachers of the Law (Matthew 23). Next, looking down on Jerusalem from the Mount of Olives, Jesus challenges his disciples' presuppositions about the future. Contrary to their expectations, Jerusalem will fall to the Romans, and his followers will face a great deal of suffering and persecution. There will also be an inevitable judgement of the world and so those who follow Jesus will have to live in a state of readiness, to 'be prepared' for his return.

These passages are a real challenge to us too. As we wait for the return of Jesus, the 'Son of Man', what sort of lives will we lead? Will he find us faithful and ready? And in a world of uncertainty, where will we place our hope? In our reputations? In the here and now? Or will Jesus find us good and faithful servants, who have placed our trust in him?

Monday
22 October

Matthew 23:1–12

Prepare to be humble

> 'For those who exalt
> themselves will be
> humbled, and those
> who humble themselves
> will be exalted.'
>
> Matthew 23:12 (NIV)

Prepare

How important is it to you that others think well of you?

Read — Matthew 23:1–12

Explore

We live in a world that's driven by individualism; a selfie-obsessed culture where people can spend considerable time creating flattering narratives about themselves on social media, competing for 'likes', attention and praise.

In this passage, Jesus doesn't mince words. He has no time for Israel's religious leaders who focus on status and seek approval from others: 'everything they do is done for people to see' (v 5), 'they love the place of honour' (v 6) and 'they love to be greeted with respect' (v 7). Worse still, they burden others with their religious decrees (v 4) based around legalism and outward displays of holiness (v 4).

Jesus' followers are to be driven by different values: 'the greatest among you will be your servant' (v 11). And we need not be burdened by rules and regulations (v 4) because we are liberated by Jesus' offer that all who come to him 'weary and burdened' will find rest for their souls; 'For my yoke is easy and my burden is light' (Matthew 11:28,29).

Respond

'Thank you, Jesus, that you have released us from rule keeping and the need to keep propping up our own egos. Help us to serve others as we live joyfully for you.'

Matthew 23:13–24

Prepare to love

Prepare

What situations of injustice are you aware of, either in today's news, or in the lives of those around you?

Read   Matthew 23:13–24

Explore

Jesus' severe language follows the conventions of an ancient polemic as he exposes the hypocrisy of the scribes and the Pharisees. What specific examples of hypocrisy does he highlight in this passage?

In their preoccupation with the minutiae (v 24), whether in taking oaths (vs 16–22) or giving away a tenth (v 23), the religious leaders have completely missed the point. Jesus has already summed up the whole goal of following the law with a command to love God and neighbour (22:37,38).

The Old Testament and the New Testament stress what's really important – justice, mercy and faithfulness (Hosea 6:6; Micah 6:8; James 1:27). The lack of justice shown by the religious teachers reveals the hollowness of their outward religious observances. In contrast, Jesus' followers, aided by the Holy Spirit, will live servant-hearted (v 11), transformed lives of faith and love.

> '*Woe to you, teachers of law and Pharisees, you hypocrites! You give a tenth of your spices ... But you have neglected the more important matters of the law – justice, mercy and faithfulness.*'
> Matthew 23:23 (NIV)

Respond

German theologian Dietrich Bonhoeffer wrote, 'Christians ... must share in Christ's large-heartedness by acting with responsibility and in freedom ... Mere waiting and looking on is not Christian behaviour. The Christian is called to sympathy and action.'* How can you show a commitment to justice and mercy in your life?

*Dietrich Bonhoeffer, *Theology of Liberation*, Diolog (Volume 34, Winter, 1995), p26

Wednesday
24 October

Matthew 23:25–36

A congruent life

> 'Blind Pharisee! First clean the inside of the cup and dish, and then the outside also will be clean.'
>
> Matthew 23:26 (NIV)

Prepare

How much does your inner life match your outer life?

Read

Matthew 23:25–36

Explore

At the end of one of his books on spiritual formation, Eugene Peterson focused on an individual who lived 'a life of congruence': someone who 'wrote what he lived (and) lived what he wrote'.* In a world where we regularly wake up to news of famous individuals whose double lives have just been exposed, there's something incredibly refreshing about Peterson's description.

Here Jesus uses shocking language to condemn the Pharisees and scribes for their lack of congruence, their hypocrisy and outer play-acting that hide inner lives of 'greed and self-indulgence', and 'wickedness' (vs 25b,28b). Religious hypocrites use religion for their own advantage, and such behaviour is condemned in the harshest terms in the Bible (v 33).

Jesus now moves to another major theme of his final teaching – the coming persecution of his followers (v 36). Jesus puts the Pharisees and scribes amongst those who have wantonly turned their backs on God's true messengers (v 31), as he faces his own inevitable persecution and death.

*Eugene Peterson, *Christ Plays in Ten Thousand Places: A Conversation in Spiritual Theology*, London, Hodder and Stoughton, 2005, p333

Respond

In following Jesus we are offered the chance for deep change and genuine inner transformation: 'the washing of rebirth and renewal by the Holy Spirit' (Titus 3:5b). Ask Jesus to transform you and to help you to live a life of congruence.

34

Bible in a Year
Jeremiah 42,43; John 16

Mercy... and judgement

Thursday
25 October

Prepare

Has there been a time in your life when someone has shown you real grace and mercy?

Read

Matthew 23:37 – 24:2

Explore

Jesus' moving lament over Jerusalem is something we need to remember as we turn to an extended and challenging section of teaching that focuses on God's judgement.

The Bible is full of passages that show God's mercy and grace: Psalm 103:8 reminds us that 'the LORD is compassionate and gracious, slow to anger, abounding in love'. Time and time again in the Bible, a loving, compassionate God withholds punishment, longing instead for a change of heart from his people who turn their backs on him. In this passage Jesus uses the maternal metaphor of a mothering bird who gathers her young under her wing (v 37) in a moving reminder of God's love and his longing for all to be reconciled to him.

And yet judgement will come. In this passage judgement is both imminent and delayed. Jesus predicts tragic events that will happen in the lifetime of his disciples (v 2), such as the fall of Jerusalem to the Roman general Titus in AD 70. But he will soon reveal that the final judgement will happen at a later date; that there will be a period of delay (Matthew 24:48b) before the return of the 'Son of Man'.

> *'Jerusalem, Jerusalem, you who kill the prophets … how often I have longed to gather your children together, as a hen gathers her chicks under her wings.'*
> Matthew 23:37 (NIV)

Respond

Thank God for his patience, mercy and compassion.

Matthew 24:3–14

ɗ

Faithful...
to the end

'... but the one who stands firm to the end will be saved.'

Matthew 24:13 (NIV)

Prepare

Have you had times in your life when you experienced the opposite of what you expected? How did you react?

Read   Matthew 24:3–14

Explore

Jesus is now talking privately to his disciples on the Mount of Olives. The group would have enjoyed a panoramic view over Jerusalem and its temple – a magnificent, imposing structure that had recently been rebuilt by Herod the Great.

Again and again the disciples are to find that their ideas of Jesus as triumphal Messiah who will dispatch the occupying Romans will differ radically from reality. Jesus has just told them the shocking news that the Temple will be destroyed. The disciples would have found it hard to dissociate the destruction of the Temple from an immediate 'end of the ages'.

Jesus stresses that nobody knows the exact time (24:36,44), but that the gospel will need to be preached to the whole world before 'the end will come' (v 14). He uses apocalyptic language to describe the 'birth pangs', or indications of the end times – wars, famines and earthquakes (vs 7,8), rumours of false messiahs (vs 4,5) and the persecution of Jesus' followers (v 9). All of these things mentioned have characterised the entire age of the church. What Jesus will now concentrate on is the importance of faithfulness, of perseverance to the end despite the cost (v 13).

Respond

Pray for the many Christians throughout the world who are currently facing intense persecution. And pray that you too will be faithful to the end.

Bible in a Year
Jeremiah 47,48; John 17

Matthew 24:15–25

Suffering...
and hope

Prepare

What are your circumstances like at the moment? Are you struggling to see God's hand in your life?

Read   Matthew 24:15–25

> 'For then there will be great distress.'
> Matthew 24:21 (NIV)

Explore

Again Jesus refers to the destruction of Jerusalem which would take place at the hands of the Romans in AD 70, after a bloody six-month siege. He warns his disciples of the horrific suffering that will be experienced in the days ahead and gives practical instructions to his disciples of how to react (v 16).

The reference to 'the abomination that causes desolation' comes straight out of the book of Daniel (12:11) and like much of this section of Matthew, uses apocalyptic, formulaic language that would have been deeply familiar to Jesus' disciples.

For Jesus' disciples the world that they knew was about to end. There would be chaos and catastrophe, with power struggles, and civil decay. The Jerusalem they knew under the 'pax Romana' (peace of Rome) would collapse and they would find themselves scattered across the known world.

And yet... despite everything, God is in control (vs 22,25). Followers of Jesus can put their faith not in some blind optimism that everything will turn out all right, but in a narrative bigger than themselves. JRR Tolkien describes Christian hope as the movement of history towards a great 'eucatastrophe' – the 'good catastrophe', a sudden joyous 'turn' that denies not the existence of sorrow and failure, but of universal, final defeat.

Respond

Read Philippians 4:12. Ask God to help you put your faith in him, and for a joy that goes beyond circumstances.

Bible in a Year
Jeremiah 49,50; John 18

Loving provision

Prepare

Have you ever resented God when you've experienced a difficulty in your life?

Read   Psalm 23

Explore

It is fitting that, after yesterday's reading about the inevitable sufferings Jesus' followers will experience, we now turn to Psalm 23 – one of the most famous psalms of all.

David – the shepherd boy who became king – refers to his old vocation to create a moving metaphor about God's loving provision and care. As shepherd, God 'leads' (v 2b), 'refreshes' (v 3), 'guides' (v 3b) and shows 'comfort' (v 4b), 'goodness' and 'love' (v 6).

This psalm does not promise a happiness that comes from an easy life. Rather it shows the comforting presence and guidance of God through a multitude of different life situations, including a walk 'through the darkest valley' (v 4b) and a meal 'in the presence of my enemies' (v 5b). Ultimately, whether the psalmist is experiencing good times or bad times, he lacks nothing (v 1) or, as another translation says, 'there is no need that God cannot fulfil'.*

The psalmist switches from using the third person, talking about God in verses 1 to 3, 'The Lord is my shepherd', to the second person from verses 4 to 6: '*you* are with me', '*you* anoint my head with oil' to show both familiarity and dependence.

*Leslie F Brandt, *Psalms Now*, Concordia Publishing House, 2004

Respond

The psalmist is not distracted by either misery or blessing because in the end God is placed at the centre of things. Ask God to help you put him in the centre of your life today, regardless of your circumstances.

All power and glory

Monday
29 October

Prepare

How do you respond to the idea of God's judgement?

Read   Matthew 24:26–35

Explore

Jesus continues to use apocalyptic language from the Old Testament book of Daniel to describe the end times, referring to himself as 'the Son of Man' (v 27b). Traditionally scholars have read this section as referring to the return of Jesus at the end of time, but others believe the highly figurative expressions used by Jesus (ie the darkening of the sun, moon and stars, v 29) describe the catastrophic times around the fall of Jerusalem.

Regardless of the timing of the events (and Jesus makes it clear that not even he knows when the end time will occur), what is implicit in this passage is the coming judgement that the Son of Man will bring about (v 31). Hence Jesus will soon move into telling a number of significant parables about the importance of watchfulness and preparedness (24:42) in the light of God's coming judgement.

In Daniel 7:14, the Son of Man is given authority, glory and power over all – by the end of Matthew (28:18) Jesus tells his disciples, 'all authority in heaven and earth has been given to me'. Jesus, soon to be crucified, will not remain defeated, for he is the glorious and exalted 'Son of Man' in whom we can place our trust.

> 'When they see the Son of Man coming on the clouds of heaven, with power and great glory.'
> Matthew 24:30b (NIV)

Respond

The spiritual realities of life are sometimes hidden but vitally important. Our response to Jesus is critical. Pray that your friends and family will put their trust in Jesus.

Matthew 24:36–44

Faithful, in the ordinary

> *'Therefore keep watch, because you do not know on what day your Lord will come.'*
>
> Matthew 24:42 (NIV)

Prepare

'When things are taking their ordinary course, it is hard to remember what matters' (Marilynne Robinson, *Gilead*, New York, Picador, 2004, p102).

Read — Matthew 24:36–44

Explore

Jesus now proceeds to use stories and parables to show the importance of readiness, even in the living of routine, ordinary life. In this parable we find individuals busy with the everyday: 'eating and drinking, marrying and giving in marriage' (v 38), working in the fields or grinding grain (vs 40,41).

Jesus compares God's sweeping unexpected judgement seen in the story of Noah and the flood with the final coming of the Son of Man (v 37). The people in these stories are living out ordinary lives. However, for some, the everyday is all there is. But for Jesus' followers, our lives are to be lived in the light of something larger than ourselves, a larger narrative (v 43). The kingdom of God has come, and while we live in the time of the 'now and not yet', both our future hope, and our status as citizens of the kingdom of God, provide ultimate meaning and give significance to the present.

Respond

Read verses 42 to 44 again. Pray that your future hope will define your outlook on life at all times, and ask God to help you to be faithful and 'watchful' in the everyday.

Matthew 24:45–51

Faithful endurance

Prepare

'Be careful not to practise your righteousness in front of others to be seen by them. If you do, you will have no reward from your Father in heaven' (Matthew 6:1).

Read   Matthew 24:45–51

Explore

Jesus now moves into a number of parables to examine different aspects of faithful living in the light of the coming judgement.

Yesterday, judgement came unexpectedly. However, in this parable there is a delay in judgement. The master puts a servant in charge of feeding a household of servants while he is away (v 45). The 'faithful and wise' servant fulfils this task in contrast to the 'wicked' servant. What does the wicked servant get up to (v 49)?

While the faithful servant is rewarded (v 47), the unfaithful servant finds himself faced with the unexpected return of his master (v 50) and faces severe punishment and 'a place with the hypocrites' (v 51). The faithful servant is wise because he has realigned his life to act as a citizen of heaven. However, like the Pharisees and Scribes that Jesus condemned in Matthew 23, the wicked servant has chosen injustice and self-indulgence. He also shows no understanding of the mercy God has shown him.

'Who then is the faithful and wise servant, whom the master has put in charge of the servants in his household to give them their food at the proper time?'
Matthew 24:45 (NIV)

Respond

A change in status means a change in behaviour: 'For you were once darkness but now you are light in the Lord. Live as children of the light … and find out what pleases the Lord' (Ephesians 5:8). Pray for God's help in living 'in the light' today.

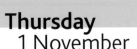

Thursday
1 November

Matthew 25:1–13

Wise waiting

> *'Therefore keep watch, because you do not know the day or the hour.'*
>
> Matthew 25:13 (NIV)

Prepare

The American writer George Saunders once made this observation: 'My sense is that we live in an incredibly material time. We like stuff, yes, but we are also inclined to think that whatever is, is all there is' (https://imagejournal.org/article/a-conversation-with-george-saunders).

Read   Matthew 25:1–13

Explore

Today's parable once again stresses the importance of how we live – because following Jesus fundamentally changes everything. We don't just live for stuff. We don't just live for the present. Our future hope imbues the present with both meaning and purpose. And this future, God's kingdom, starts from the moment we follow Jesus.

Jesus uses the metaphor of a wedding to look at the importance of faithful kingdom living, and again it focuses on a bridegroom who is later than expected (v 5). The ten bridesmaids all do the same thing – they fall asleep (v 5)! Yet once again there is a subtle difference in behaviour: some are 'wise' and some are 'foolish' (v 2). The 'wise' bridesmaids are both expectant and prepared for a delay, armed with sufficient oil for their lamps (v 7). A lack of oil for the foolish bridesmaids shows an unpreparedness for the coming of the bridegroom (v 8).

Once again Jesus is talking about the necessity of faithful preparedness even in the everyday, mundane events of life. There is to be a shift in attitude for Jesus' followers, a different outlook.

Respond

In reality, are you living as if the present is all there is? Ask God to help you see your life from a different perspective.

42

Bible in a Year
Ezekiel 2,3; Psalm 119:97–120

Matthew 25:14–30

Wise stewardship

Prepare

What do you think getting on with God's work in his world looks like for you?

Read

Matthew 25:14–30

Explore

Again Jesus uses a parable to look at what 'readiness' looks like. What is emphasised is a conscious obedience in the use of the master's resources, or 'stewardship'.

The three servants in this parable are each given different amounts of gold to 'steward' while the master is away (v 14). In the end, the amount given to each servant is somewhat irrelevant (v 15). What is significant in this parable is what the servants *do* with what has been given to them (v 19). Clear here is Jesus' demand that we put to good use whatever gifts he has given us.

The third servant buries the bag of gold entrusted to him (v 18), but when confronted with his lack of faithfulness he blames the master (v 24b) as a 'hard man'. His motivation is fear, not trust.

The idea of a lived-out faith that trusts in the goodness of God and 'bears fruit' is crucial in the Gospels. Jesus says, 'No one lights a lamp and hides it in a clay jar or puts it under a bed' (Luke 8:16). This parable is not about buying your salvation but it does emphasise that the good news of the coming of the kingdom of God should be life-changing. The two faithful servants receive further blessing, but the unfaithful servant loses even that which he has been blessed with (v 29).

> *'His master replied, "Well done, good and faithful servant! You have been faithful with a few things; I will put you in charge of many things …"'*
> Matthew 25:23 (NIV)

Respond

Ask God to help you to be a faithful 'steward' of all that he has given you.

Matthew 25:31–46

Living faith

Prepare

Spend some time thinking and praying about what this verse means for how you treat those around you: 'We love because he first loved us' (1 John 4:19).

Read   Matthew 25:31–46

Explore

Here the judgement day has arrived and Jesus the 'Son of Man' is both King (v 34) and Lord. He comes 'in his glory' (v 31) with the nations gathered at his throne (v 32). And who are the blessed? Those who have taken seriously the ultimate love command of the Law (see, for example, Matthew 7:12; 22:36–39; 23:23). Earlier in Matthew Jesus has extended this love command to even our enemies (Matthew 5:43,44).

Jesus' faithful servants have given food to the hungry (v 35), clothes to those without (v 36), visited the sick and those in prison and provided hospitality to the stranger (v 36). Even more radical is the idea that 'Whatever you did for one of the least of these … you did for me' (v 40).

We started our series with Jesus attacking the religious leaders of Jerusalem for their hypocrisy, for their insistence on being seen and noticed and important. We finish Jesus' final discourse with a great reversal. Those who are the outsiders, the unimportant, the forgotten, are remembered according to the values of the kingdom of God. And once again Jesus stresses that loving God is all about loving one's neighbour.

Respond

Ask God to fill you with love for others, and to open your eyes to the needy around you.

Bible in a Year
Ezekiel 6,7; James 2

Goodness and mercy

Prepare

When you read of 'the fear of the Lord', how does this make you feel?

Read

Psalm 25

> *The LORD confides in those who fear him; he makes his covenant known to them.*
>
> Psalm 25:14 (NIV)

Explore

There are times in our lives where we are not sure of the path ahead, times where we may be betrayed by those we love, or overwhelmed by difficult circumstances.

This psalm finds David in anguish (v 17b): lonely, afflicted, distressed (vs 16,18) and surrounded by his enemies (vs 2,19). David does not hide behind false, spiritual clichés, but instead he is brutally honest about his worries and insecurities.

Reacting to his circumstances, he reminds himself of the goodness of God (v 7b) – a God who exhibits mercy and love (v 6) – and he puts himself in God's hands (v 15). David asks God for guidance, to 'show me your paths' (v 4) and 'guide me in your truth'. And David doesn't only point the blame at those wishing him harm. He has a realistic view of himself, and is aware of his own wrongdoing and brokenness (vs 7,11,18b).

Ultimately he stresses the importance of the 'fear of the Lord'. Eugene Peterson describes this as a posture whereby we 'interrupt our preoccupation with ourselves and attend to God'.* Fear of the Lord requires humility (v 9) and dependence, but ultimately it also brings us closer to the one who made us (v 14).

Respond

Are you battling worries and insecurities? Pray through this psalm, putting your life in God's hands and asking him to show you a way forward.

*Eugene Peterson, *Christ Plays in Ten Thousand Places: A Conversation in Spiritual Theology*, London, Hodder and Stoughton, 2005, p43

Judgement and promise

Writer

Andy Bathgate

Andy is married to Alyson and they live in Edinburgh where they are elders in Craiglockhare Church of Scotland. They love spending time with their two grandsons, visiting art galleries and reading.

The twin ideas of judgement and promise are prominent throughout the book and in these chapters. The God of promise binds himself in commitment with the words, 'I will be their God, and they will be my people' (31:33). But the same God also speaks words of severe judgement on his people, on Babylon (ch 51) and on surrounding nations (chs 46–51). The appalling image of dead bodies in 33:5 is God's people, slain by the Lord. But promise never dies. If judgement does its work, humbling and disciplining and leading to repentance, then the promise of forgiveness is available (36:3). God will work, even with the few, to fulfil his purpose (44:14,28).

The historical background to these chapters are the events from around the fall of Jerusalem to the invading Babylonian army. But we start in a very different place with the Book of Consolation (chs 30–33). This is a series of spectacular images and astounding promises that don't ignore the indignity of exile but bring comforting words of restoration and hope (eg 33:8,9). There is then a major focus on the word of the Lord and responses to it. Jeremiah fearlessly speaks the word only to see it treated with disdain (ch 36) and disbelief (ch 39). Leadership's response to God's word has huge implications for the direction of the community. With the close of the book comes confirmation that the Lord's word has been fulfilled. If the word of judgement comes true, we can completely trust the promises of restoration, fulfilled in Jesus.

Jeremiah 31:1–22

Future proof?

Prepare

'… no human mind has conceived "the things God has prepared for those who love him" – these are the things God has revealed to us by his Spirit' (1 Corinthians 2:9,10). Give thanks for what God has prepared for us.

Read   Jeremiah 31:1–22

Explore

No one image can capture God's restoring work. So, when Jeremiah, after many prophecies of judgement, pens his 'Book of Consolation' (chs 30–33), he plunders a whole bank of images to reinforce his message: that God loves his people and will renew them. It recalls but surpasses the Exodus.

God's commitment to his people means that despite their waywardness (vs 18,19) and their disabilities (v 8) he will bring them to a settled home. In the New Testament, Paul calls us to trust the same God, who is determined to complete the work he has started in us (Philippians 1:6). For those of us broken by our sin, or the sin of others, there is still hope. God never lets go until he completes the restoration (v 20). Here also is the prospect of a fertile place (v 12) for those whose present surroundings are a barren wilderness (v 2). Our present experience may be one of frustration and tears, but our imaginations need to be fired by images of future security and exuberant joy (eg vs 4,7,9,12,13). Singing is a major feature of Jeremiah's vision. The only tears are those of joy. Catastrophe can turn to blessing in God's hands (vs 15,16).

> *The LORD appeared to us in the past, saying: 'I have loved you with an everlasting love; I have drawn you with unfailing kindness.'*
> Jeremiah 31:3 (NIV)

Respond

How do you respond to Jeremiah's idyllic vision? Try to identify signs of God's restoration in your Christian community. Give thanks for these indicators of the coming universal transformation.

Bible in a Year
Ezekiel 10,11; James 3

47

Tuesday
6 November

Jeremiah 31:27–40

If it's broken, it needs fixing

> *'This is the covenant that I will make with the people of Israel after that time,' declares the LORD. 'I will put my law in their minds and write it on their hearts. I will be their God, and they will be my people.'*
>
> Jeremiah 31:33 (NIV)

Prepare

What present issues or past failures hinder your approach to God? Hear the comforting words of Jesus – 'your sins are forgiven' – spoken to you. Express your gratitude with liberty.

Read   Jeremiah 31:27–40

Explore

'Everything is broken' (Bob Dylan, 1989). We easily identify with Bob Dylan's take on society. God's future involves restoring the ruined and the dysfunctional. There is a judgement day of overthrow and destruction (v 28) but also a day of building and planting. God demolishes to build something new and fresh. The promise, 'I will be their God, and they will be my people' (v 33) underlines that God's fresh new thing is primarily about relationship and community. Its scope is illustrated by the reuniting of both parts of the divided kingdoms of Israel and Judah (vs 27,31) and its ultimate embracing of both Jew and Gentile (see Ephesians 3:6).

God had been a husband to the people of Israel (v 32). They had reneged on their vows. The relationship was in tatters; yet God refuses to walk away (v 36). But neither is he content with the status quo. A new covenant with deeper and stronger relational bonds will be initiated – internalised (v 33); intimate (v 34a), unrestricted (v 34b) and accessible (v 34c) but carrying greater personal accountability (v 30). Jesus is the mediator of this 'superior covenant', which is 'established on better promises' (see Hebrews 8:6). This is our heritage, our purpose, our hope.

Respond

God's work builds relationship and community (a city, 'holy to the Lord', v 40). Pray for the purity and unity of the church, locally and nationally. What is your role in building unity?

48

Bible in a Year
Ezekiel 12,13; James 4

Can dead bones live?

Prepare

'Almighty God, whose will is to restore all things in your well-beloved son. Mercifully grant that the peoples of the earth, divided and enslaved by sin, may be freed and brought together under his most gracious rule' (*Book of Common Prayer*).

Read   Jeremiah 33:1–26

Explore

'Now it is empty, without people or animals. But when that time comes, shepherds will take care of their flocks in pastures near every town …'
Jeremiah 33:12 (CEV)

The word of the Lord comes to Jeremiah while under arrest. Accused of collaboration with the Babylonians, he is imprisoned by Zedekiah. But God's word cannot be chained, even when his servants suffer frustrating and unfair restrictions (see Philippians 1:12). God's word brings with it an invitation to uncover 'great and unsearchable things' (v 3). Submissive believers grasp mysteries hidden from the greatest minds, gaining insight into God's eternal purpose (see Ephesians 1:9–14).

Revelation from God can be exceedingly uncomfortable. Who wants to hear about streets 'littered with dead bodies' or God's 'disgust' (v 5, *The Message*)? Can a place of such abandonment become a place of health and healing (v 6)? Can it become a light to the world (v 9)? Recall 'desolate' China, Nepal and Cambodia where salvation's songs of joy and gladness (v 11) have rung out in recent decades! Jeremiah's rich images test our faith. Small beginnings (v 15) lead to the re-establishment of the line of kings and priests that ensure godly leadership and access to a merciful God. We see Jesus; our prophet, priest and king.

Respond

How is your expectation of God affected by this passage? Are there people or cultures you have written off as just too hard? Cry out to God.

Thursday
8 November

Cut it out!

Prepare

Use this prayer to focus on your reading of Scripture: 'Give us the grace to receive your word with reverence and humility, without which no one can understand your truth' (John Calvin).

Read Jeremiah 36:1–32

Explore

God's words of judgement are mostly conditional. They carry a yearning that the threat of judgement will alert people to danger and generate a reaction; repentance readily met with forgiveness (v 3). Jeremiah writes harsh words out of compassion, like the renowned preacher Robert Murray McCheyne who, on hearing his friend had preached on hell, inquired, 'Did you preach it with tears?'

Speaking the word of God always provokes various reactions. Jeremiah's words, spoken by Baruch, are initially taken seriously (v 15), provoking fear (v 16). In striking contrast, King Jehoiakim and his officials show not a shred of fear (v 24). As leaders they are too proud to listen; characteristic of many leaders who struggle to admit they are wrong. Arrogance closes off ears from hearing the warning of coming disaster. Important leadership lessons emerge; the necessity of humility, resisting the temptation to silence one's critics (v 26) but above all, the consequences for many of the folly of a few. Jehoiakim's ungodly leadership brings calamity not just on himself (v 30) but on all the people (v 31). The word of God cannot be banned, burned or ignored. It 'endures for ever' (see Isaiah 40:8).

Respond

Pray that you will speak God's word today with all confidence and deep compassion. Do you tend to over-emphasise one of these elements? How do you need to change?

Bible in a Year
Ezekiel 16,17; Psalm 119:145–176

Jeremiah 38:1–28

Fake news?

Prepare

Give thanks for Jesus, who boldly 'made the good confession' before Pontius Pilate, not shirking the ensuing humiliation and suffering (1 Timothy 6:13).

Read   Jeremiah 38:1–28

Explore

Imagine Winston Churchill's famous 'Fight them on the beaches' speech being rewritten to say: 'We will not defend our island, we'll give way on our beaches, hand over our fields. We will surrender.' It would have provoked a national outcry. Jeremiah's task is to convey a traitor's message, discouraging resistance (v 4). God is no longer fighting for his people. They must take their discipline. What a counterintuitive and culturally insensitive message; not unlike Christian truth being spoken in the public square of contemporary nations or even God's word being unleashed amongst us as compromised believers. Jeremiah is no pacifist. This is non-resistance to enable God's refining judgement.

Speaking the word of God is costly for one's reputation and for one's health (vs 4,6). Are we ready for that cost? Some, like Jeremiah, are called to speak truth to power. If you are looking for acclaim this may not be for you! Jeremiah's suffering is amplified because of the weak leadership of King Zedekiah (v 5). He stands in line with Darius the Mede (Daniel), Herod (John the Baptist) and Pilate (Jesus) as weak kings who abused power to wrongly condemn adversaries. We are grateful for a leader who specialises in humble service.

> *Jeremiah replied, 'You won't be handed over to them if you choose to obey the LORD. Your life will be spared, and all will go well for you.'*
> Jeremiah 38:20 (NLT)

Respond

What should you speak out about in your community and nation? Pray for leaders in church and nation, and especially for Christians in the public arena.

Jeremiah 39:1–18

Is anyone there?

> *'I will save you; you will not fall by the sword but will escape with your life, because you trust in me, declares the LORD.'*
>
> Jeremiah 39:18 (NIV)

Prepare

'O loving wisdom of our God! When all was sin and shame. A second Adam to the fight, and to the rescue came' (JH Newman, 1865). Give thanks that Jesus has broken the power of darkness.

Read   Jeremiah 39:1–18

Explore

Here is a story of sharp contrasts. God's mission of salvation comes with inevitable judgement. It's a story of rich and poor, of destruction contrasted with protection, of humiliation and honouring, of faithfulness and infidelity. King Zedekiah as leader bears responsibility for the state of the nation. He is soundly defeated, his household despoiled, his palace destroyed and he himself humiliated. Shorn of power, he is taken into captivity as God had warned. The proud are brought low as God's judgement begins with his own household (see 1 Peter 4:17). Far from being immune to his searching judgement, God's people stand first in line. Greater privileges carry greater responsibilities.

In contrast, the poorest people in Judah are left; Jeremiah is honoured by the Babylonians and Ebed-Melek, the original Ethiopian eunuch (38:7, ESV), is favoured by God (v 18). He demonstrated his trust in God by siding with Jeremiah and therefore with God's word (see Jeremiah 38:7–13). Amid the chaos of evil, God still had his people, even when it seemed no one was left. God can use anyone to accomplish his purpose, even Babylonians who do not recognise the Lord, but he looks for faithful people.

Respond

Do you ever feel isolated as a follower of Jesus? Many do, not least young Christians in schools. Pray about this, drawing on today's passage.

Bible in a Year
Ezekiel 20,21; 1 Peter 2

Psalm 26

Blessed assurance

Prepare

Draw near to God now with 'full assurance' of faith, cleansed from a 'guilty conscience' (Hebrews 10:22). Is anything hindering you? Jesus has opened the way through his blood.

Read   Psalm 26

Lord, I love the house where you live, the place where your glory dwells.
Psalm 26:8 (NIV)

Explore

David's claims don't sit right with us. He's a bit too self-satisfied and boastful. He defends himself, sure of his clear conscience before God and other people. Could we ever adopt that approach? It's important to understand that David does not claim perfection. His contention is that he is loyal, no matter the peer pressure (vs 4,5). His allegiance to God is demonstrated in his trust in God's unfailing love and reliance on God's faithfulness (v 3). He is as dependent on God's mercy as any of us (v 11). But his trust gives him great confidence.

The Lord sees our hearts. He knows when they are aligned with his; when his glory is our chief concern (v 8). He looks for a Timothy who looks out not for his own interests but for those of Jesus Christ (Philippians 2:21), or for a Persis, a 'woman who has worked very hard in the Lord' (Romans 16:12). Living like that produces 'great assurance' in faith (1 Timothy 3:13). Perhaps David's experience is not so foreign after all. When we are accused, misrepresented, or have our integrity called into question, we too can come with a clear conscience before God and ask for vindication.

Respond

How honest are you with God about how you feel? Speak openly to him now.

Jeremiah 40:1 – 41:3

Messy church

> 'GOD came and did what he had warned he'd do because you all sinned against GOD and wouldn't do what he told you. So now you're all suffering the consequences.'
>
> Jeremiah 40:3
> (*The Message*)

Prepare

'You are a sinner, a great, desperate sinner; now come as the sinner you are, to the God who loves you' (Dietrich Bonhoeffer, *Life Together*, 1954). We mess up; God never gives up.

Read   Jeremiah 40:1 – 41:3

Explore

There is great irony in the juxtaposition of Jeremiah gaining freedom while his fellow nationals are carted off in chains to captivity. Most notably, King Zedekiah is now in shackles (39:7). The prophet and the word of God are vindicated. There is also considerable embarrassment that the Babylonian commander seems to have a clearer understanding of the Exile than the people of God (vs 2–4). It echoes the Roman soldier and Canaanite woman displaying greater faith than God's people (Matthew 8:10; 15:22), foreshadowing the drawing of Gentiles into God's purposes.

God is at work, correcting wrongs and punishing evil. Even an embryonic return from exile emerges (v 12). But sin is also still at work, disrupting a fragile but promising opportunity for peace (vs 9,10). An episode of intrigue and skulduggery ends in the assassination of the Babylonian appointee, Gedaliah. Such is the messiness of human relations, engaging in conflict when peace is within our grasp. God's work in this world is only a foretaste of the glory to come, but it is always interrupted by human stupidity. Think of Peter, before a transfigured Christ, ruining the moment by failing to grasp the uniqueness of Jesus.

Respond

Our lives in church and community are constantly afflicted by failures. How do you handle that for yourself and in relation to others? Are you too hard or too soft? How does God view these failures?

Bible in a Year
Ezekiel 24,25; 1 Peter 3

Mind games

Prepare

'Set your sights on the realities of heaven, where Christ sits in the place of honour at God's right hand ... Think about the things of heaven' (Colossians 3:1,2, NLT). Allow your mind to be enthralled with spiritual realities.

Read   Jeremiah 41:16 – 42:22

> 'I told the people: You escaped the disaster that struck Judah, but now the LORD warns you to stay away from Egypt.'
> Jeremiah 42:19 (CEV)

Explore

There is a constant tussle going on for the hearts and minds of God's people. A desire to know God's guidance can be overwhelmed by fear that obedience will be costly and painful. God's word can seem way out of kilter with the way we have been schooled to think by our society. Jeremiah and the people face that predicament. God says: 'Don't go to Egypt' when everything else says: 'It's wisest and safest to seek protection in Egypt' (42:14). It's a no-brainer. What would you have done?

The decision is a life and death issue. The Egypt option is so attractive, but it's a death trap (vs 16,17). Deuteronomy, which may inform Jeremiah's words, puts it starkly: setting a choice between life and prosperity against death and destruction (Deuteronomy 30:15–20). Is this what is at stake in responding to the voice of God? Egypt may possibly also act figuratively as a return to slavery. In the New Testament, Paul is astonished at the thought that Galatian Christians, freed by the grace of God, will turn back to slavery (see Galatians 4:8–12). It's deadly to lose freedom in Christ.

Respond

Do you view your Bible engagement as a life and death issue? How would you explain that idea to a recent follower of Jesus?

Bible in a Year
Ezekiel 26,27; 1 Peter 4

Jeremiah 43:1–13

Are you receiving me?

Prepare

'When all you owned was taken from you, you accepted it with joy' (Hebrews 10:34, NLT). Ponder how one arrives at such a mindset. Pray for your mind to be moulded to be like that.

Read   Jeremiah 43:1–13

So Johanan son of Kareah and all the army officers and all the people disobeyed the LORD's command to stay in the land of Judah.

Jeremiah 43:4 (NIV)

Explore

How receptive are you to God's word? There are times when 'the word of the Lord' runs counter to our common sense and even seems to threaten our well-being (v 3). A posture of arrogance (v 2) sets us up as the arbiters of truth. We may not shout 'liar' at the preacher but when we deny forgiveness to those who hurt us, fail to love the irritating, or refuse to say 'sorry', it is much the same thing. That refusal to listen has huge consequences for leaders and followers alike (v 5). It has consequences for Jeremiah who is dragged into the disobedience of going to Egypt (v 7). He has no choice in his location, but he can choose the inclination of his heart. And that is towards God (v 8).

In Egypt, Jeremiah performs a prophetic act. He declares God's intention to use his 'servant' Nebuchadnezzar to shatter Egyptian power and with it his own people. The people who should have been the remnant to start God's reseeding of the land lie defeated in Egypt. The restoration will have to wait for people who will listen to God. A people remaining faithful, 'even though it meant terrible suffering' (Hebrews 10:32, NLT).

Respond

We want to keep ourselves and our churches alert to the word of the Lord. What enhances that alertness and what dowses enthusiasm?

Bible in a Year
Ezekiel 28,29; 1 Peter 5

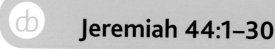

Jeremiah 44:1–30

Relegated God

Prepare

'You shall have no other gods before me' (Exodus 20:3). Acknowledge the Lord of all; your only hope and second to none.

Read Jeremiah 44:1–30

Explore

Idolatry lies at the root of disobedience. For the Jews seeking refuge in Egypt, idol worship produced a breathtaking arrogance, severing dependence on God and resulting in flagrant disobedience (vs 15–17). It's inherent to our humanity to worship something. But when we squander our worship on things other than God it disfigures us (v 8) and displaces the only one who can give us purpose. We convince ourselves that idols are fundamental to true happiness and prosperity (v 18). It's why we crave success, desire more and flashier possessions, seek sexual satisfaction and the perfect family. We think that these can afford us security (v 17) when seeking them can bring down divine retribution (vs 27,28).

Could this passage be any more pointed about the effect of idolatry on the Lord? When he is displaced from his rightful position it provokes a huge reaction. It's not just a pity we set up our idols, it is deadly (v 26). We are well warned. Yet, even here there is hope. Idolatry brings complete destruction, almost! The phrases 'except a few fugitives' (v 14) and the 'very few' (who return to Judah) (v 28) underscore that God is not finished with his people. He still has a gracious purpose.

> 'Why arouse my anger with what your hands have made, burning incense to other gods in Egypt, where you have come to live? You will destroy yourselves and make yourselves a curse and an object of reproach among all the nations on earth.'
> Jeremiah 44:8 (NIV)

Respond

What steps do you need to take to ensure idolatry does not displace God and lead to arrogant disobedience in your life?

Bible in a Year
Ezekiel 30,31; Psalms 123–125

Friday
16 November

Plot spoiler?

'My people, I am on your side, and I will take revenge on Babylon. I will cut off its water supply, and its stream will dry up.'
Jeremiah 51:36 (CEV)

Prepare

What causes you the greatest anxiety and fear? Bring it into the open before the Sovereign Lord who reigns over history and wants only your good.

Read   Jeremiah 51:33–64

Explore

God, the Lord Almighty, must eventually exert his reign. All oppressors and everything that sets itself up in opposition to God must finally succumb to his control. The Babylonian Empire seems impenetrable with its thick walls and high gates (v 58). But even its strength, power and sophistication must bend to his power. The walls will fall (v 44), just as in time, every knee will bow to another Lord, Jesus Christ (see Philippians 2:10). But prior to that, evil will be in the ascendancy. God's people will be 'devoured' (v 34) and 'disgraced' (v 51); holy places defiled (v 51). It is no surprise that Babylon, with its arrogance and boastfulness (v 41), in the book of Revelation becomes the personification of opposition to God and his plans. The extent of its power is not hidden from us, even describing the saints being conquered (Revelation 13:7). This is ferocious opposition, so that one might even call into question God's ability to intervene. But God will always defend the cause of his people (v 36). We are his and his glory is to be displayed through us. We must flee evil (vs 45–48) but never lose heart or be afraid. The outcome is never in doubt.

Respond

Why does God tolerate 'Babylon-type' behaviour? You may not have a complete answer, but you can pray for the overthrow of Babylon-type behaviour in our world and for the protection of God's people.

Bible in a Year
Ezekiel 32,33; 2 Peter 1

Jeremiah 52:1–34

A flickering candle

Prepare

'At midnight I rise to give you thanks for your righteous laws' (Psalm 119:62). Consider how much you resonate with the psalmist.

Read   Jeremiah 52:1–34

So Judah went into captivity, away from her land.
Jeremiah 52:27b

Explore

This final chapter provides a summary of the causes and the outcomes of the Exile. It is a sad story of the decline of a nation, of rebellion against love, and of God's judgement on his people (v 3). The destruction of Judah is completed. Solomon's Temple, and all it conveyed about God's glory dwelling amongst them, is burned down. The priests and sacrificial implements that enabled the people to draw near to God in worship are removed (vs 17–23). This is the end, or so it seems. Yet the book somehow ends on an upbeat note. Jehoiachin is freed and honoured during exile in Babylon (vs 32–34). And so, the book ends, with God's people under judgement and foreign rule, but acknowledged during their time of banishment. There is a sign of hope even in this darkest hour.

God allows all this to happen (even orchestrating much of it), just as he has overseen the rise of every challenge to his rule and every attempt to neuter his people – right up to today. Part of God's judgement is to withdraw his restraining influence (see Romans 1:24–26), whilst longing that people will repent (see Romans 2:4). There is hope that God and his people, even in exile, will be honoured.

Respond

As you do the usual things of life, what difference does it make that we know a God of judgement and hope?

Psalm 27

Your greatest fear

My heart says of you, 'Seek his face!' Your face, LORD, I will seek.
Psalm 27:8 (NIV)

Prepare

'Fear Him, ye saints, and you will then have nothing else to fear' (N Brady and N Tate, 1696). Reflect on what fearing God means for you. Does it banish other fears?

Read   Psalm 27

Explore

It's one thing to rejoice in God in the good times, when the sun is shining, and everything is harmonious. It's quite another to remain steady when under threat; being accused and feeling abandoned by those closest to you. David somehow manages to keep his head, calling his listeners to patient waiting and resilience (v 14). He does it by keeping his heart fixed on the Lord (v 8). The temptation is to look elsewhere; to the threat posed by wicked people (v 2); to war waged against him (v 3); to possible breakdown of relationships (v 10).

These could all, understandably, be causes for deep anxiety and for throwing in the towel. It's not all water off a duck's back to David. He feels the strain, crying to the Lord not to forsake him (v 9). But as he faces up to all the potential pitfalls, he reminds himself at every turn that 'the one who is in you is greater than the one who is in the world' (1 John 4:4). Fear is bred in the darkness but God is David's light. Snarling evil contrasts with the Lord's beauty. The Lord's goodness overwhelms all malice. Nothing can separate us from God's love in Christ (Romans 8:35). So, hang on in there.

Respond

Fear of others and of the future dictates much of our lives. What can you do to get these fears into perspective for yourself and others?

Bible in a Year
Ezekiel 36,37; Psalms 126–128

Fresh bread, out now!

Don't miss your new look January – March 2019 issue of *Daily Bread*, available from early December.

Fresh next issue:

Ron Frost
on 1 Kings

Elaine Duncan
on 1 Peter

Emlyn Williams
on Acts

How to order

- through your local Christian bookshop
- by phone: 01908 856 006
- by fax: 01908 856 020
- by post: Freepost SU MAIL ORDER
- through your church Bible-reading representative

Or why not subscribe?

See inside the back cover for more details on how to subscribe to *Daily Bread*.

Strong
and stable

Writer

Jonathan Gemmell

Jonathan is Associate Director of Conferences and Resources with the Proclamation Trust in London.

'Strong and stable' will forever be the infamous slogan of the Conservative Party in the 2017 UK General Election. However, it is also a great summary of 2 Timothy and Titus.

Paul is writing to two of his gifted lieutenants who trained under him over a number of years. The apostolic age is soon to end and it is these younger church leaders who are now called to guard, preach, suffer for and adorn the gospel.

Timothy is in Ephesus. He faces significant pressures from within the church where people are teaching what should not be taught. Paul writes to say, stay 'strong'.

On the other hand, Paul says to Titus that he is to 'stabilise' the church. Titus is to put in order the things left unfinished, to set up leadership in the church. Titus is to make the Cretan church stable.

These two letters are written to church leaders about church leadership but they are good for all of us: **1)** All the qualities listed for leaders are applied to every believer elsewhere in the New Testament. **2)** The congregation are the safety net, ensuring church leaders stay on course. **3)** These letters help us pray well for our church leaders. **4)** No church leader stays forever, so understanding these letters helps us know what to look for when vacancies arise. **5)** These letters are brimming with Jesus.

My prayer is that over the next fortnight, you will be strengthened and stabilised through faith in Jesus Christ.

You are family

Prepare

Think about all the people who were involved in teaching you about Jesus. Why not pray and give thanks to God for each of these people now?

Read   2 Timothy 1:1–7

Explore

How many different relationships are listed in these seven verses? At the start of this very personal letter, Paul is reminding Timothy of the rich history that has brought them to this point: Timothy's history in hearing the gospel (v 5), and Paul and Timothy's history together (vs 2–4). At the start of this letter aimed at strengthening Timothy for his leadership role, Paul takes time to anchor Timothy's story.

This is all important because in verses 6 and 7 we get the overarching command of the letter, that Timothy is to 'fan into flame the gift of God'. In other words, Timothy is to lead the Ephesian church with everything he has got, not smouldering away or petering out, but giving his all, fanning into flame his ministry. Paul reminds Timothy he is not alone – God by his indwelling Spirit strengthens him for the task at hand.

> *For the Spirit God gave us does not make us timid, but gives us power, love and self-discipline.*
> 2 Timothy 1:7 (NIV)

Respond

Thinking about your own life and walk with Jesus, spend some time asking God to help you share your faith with others, and asking that with the Spirit's help, you might grow in love and service for the Lord Jesus.

Ashamed?

> *May the Lord grant that he will find mercy from the Lord on that day! You know very well in how many ways he helped me in Ephesus.*
>
> 2 Timothy 1:18 (NIV)

Prepare

When are you most tempted to be ashamed of Jesus? When is it that you want to distance yourself from the truth and claim of the gospel?

Read   2 Timothy 1:8–18

Explore

What are the twin commands in verse 8? How are they connected? In this dense section of the letter Paul reminds Timothy of the nature of the gospel (vs 9,10), Paul's ministry for the gospel (vs 11,12) and Timothy's part in the work of the gospel (vs 8,13,14). It is a rich tapestry with the overall message being that gospel work brings suffering and hardship now, but certain hope of glory in the end. It is a call to stick with Jesus, which means sticking with Paul.

You can see from verses 15 to 18 that the prospect of suffering and the hardship of belonging to Jesus has not been embraced by many. In fact, due to shame and suffering connected with the gospel, everyone in the province of Asia has deserted Paul (v 15). People checked out when the sparks started flying. Onesiphorus stands in stark contrast, one who didn't distance himself from Paul and the gospel but actively sought out Paul in prison to support and strengthen him.

Respond

In different ways, every situation in life can challenge our commitment to Jesus and our faithfulness to the gospel. Today, are we willing to suffer for Jesus, being unashamed in the face of scorn, like Onesiphorus? Pray for courage, strength and a steadfast love for Jesus.

2 Timothy 2:1–13

Gospel work is hard work

Prepare

What are some of the hardest occupations? Which jobs require discipline, focus, perseverance and hard labour?

Read   2 Timothy 2:1–13

Explore

Think about what would be in a job description for a soldier, an athlete and a farmer. What qualities do each of them need?

Paul here uses these occupations to paint a picture of what qualities Timothy needs for his ministry. The soldier is single-minded, focused purely on obeying and serving his commander. The athlete is disciplined, hard-working and law-abiding. The farmer is patient, diligent and invested. These are the qualities Timothy needs to do his work.

All of these jobs have the hope of glory in the end – the work pays off. The soldier is on the winning side, the athlete gains the victor's crown, the farmer reaps a harvest. Hard work now but glory later. This is how Paul is encouraging Timothy in this section of the letter, telling him gospel work is hard work but in the end it will be more than worth it.

In verse 8 he shows this shape of ministry in the life of the Lord Jesus – the King who went through death to receive his crown. And Paul also endures now in the sure and certain hope of eternal glory in the end (v 10).

> *You then, my son, be strong in the grace that is in Christ Jesus.*
> 2 Timothy 2:1 (NIV)

Respond

Pray for your church leaders and yourself that you would have this perspective as you serve Jesus. Pray you would know that though gospel work is hard work, it brings eternal glory.

2 Timothy 2:14–26

Teach, avoid, correct

Keep reminding God's people of these things. Warn them before God against quarrelling about words; it is of no value, and only ruins those who listen.

2 Timothy 2:14 (NIV)

Prepare

What is the most important task in gospel ministry? Of all the things pastors and ministers do, what should they prioritise?

Read   2 Timothy 2:14–26

Explore

In this section Paul gives Timothy three clear pointers of what his work is to involve.

First (vs 14,15), Timothy is to teach God's people correctly. His ministry is to be one of being an unashamed workman who clearly, fully and devotedly gives himself to teaching God's Word. If your church leaders do that, give thanks for them now.

Secondly, he is to teach the truth because there is so much falsehood around. Those like Hymenaeus and Philetus (v 17) are destroying people with their gangrenous teaching, proclaiming that the resurrection has already happened (v 18). Timothy is to avoid such error and boldly proclaim what is true. Teaching truth is the best weapon to tackle falsehood.

Thirdly, he is to correct error. Timothy is not to be bristling for arguments, quarrels and clashes over irrelevancies. The people who are confused about the truth are to be gently instructed (v 25).

Timothy is to focus on faithfully teaching God's Word, and as he does this people will grow, falsehood will be exposed and error will be corrected.

Respond

Think about your church. Is the ministry that goes on there in line with what you have read today? Pray that God's Word would be handled correctly, preached and taught faithfully.

Bible in a Year
Ezekiel 44,45; Psalms 129–131

2 Timothy 3:1–9

Friday
23 November

Dark days ahead

Prepare

Father God, help me stay faithful to your Son Jesus, help me see and avoid falsehood and keep me in your truth.'

Read   2 Timothy 3:1–9

Explore

Paul has reminded Timothy to teach the Bible, and now he warns him that things will get worse. There will be terrible days full of terrible people ahead. There will be people peddling a counterfeit Christianity that will prey on the vulnerable and gullible. From this passage, what will it look like?

These people will exhibit a sham Christianity that is both permissive and poisonous. Their loves are totally disordered (vs 2–4) and their 'godliness' is a sham (v 5). It will be the weak and vulnerable who will be swept up in the charade (vs 6,7). Paul is warning Timothy so he will faithfully teach the truth as a means of protecting his people from all these lies.

This counterfeit Christianity will not survive forever though; Paul makes reference to the Pharaoh's sorcerers in the book of Exodus who were only able to copy Moses' signs and wonders for so long, before their game was up. So even in these dark days, Timothy is to have great hope that the truth he teaches will outlast the fraud.

But mark this: there will be terrible times in the last days.
2 Timothy 3:1 (NIV)

Respond

Take time to think about people you know who have been carried away by false teaching. Pray for them. Think about new Christians you know and pray they might love the truth and grow in it, and not be deceived by error and falsehood.

Saturday
24 November

2 Timothy 3:10–17
All-sufficient Scripture

All Scripture is God-breathed and is useful for teaching, rebuking, correcting and training in righteousness ...

2 Timothy 3:16 (NIV)

Prepare

What is the Bible for? Make a list of all the things you can think of.

Read   2 Timothy 3:10–17

Explore

Paul tells Timothy (v 10) to live a life that contrasts sharply with the lives of the false teachers (vs 1–9). Timothy is to continue to imitate Paul, aiming for the same perseverance and continuing in his pattern of ministry and endurance (v 14). This is a way of life that is opposed to the evildoers and imposters of verse 13. Timothy is to live a consistent Christian life, even though those around him may go from bad to worse, going deeper into their deception. He is to continue in the biblical and apostolic gospel without being distracted or deflected by anything else.

Timothy's ministry is to be one rooted in Scripture. Make a list of all the things that the Scriptures can do in verses 15 and 16.

Timothy has a difficult task to accomplish in Ephesus. But, in God's all-sufficient Word he has everything he needs to accomplish the task he has been given. The all-sufficient Word provides a thorough equipping for every good work for the whole congregation (vs 17).

Respond

'Father God, help me to love your Word, delight in your Word, feast on your Word, meditate on your Word. Father, help me be one who is thoroughly equipped for every good work through your all-sufficient Word. Cultivate in my life an appetite that craves your Word above all things.'

Psalm 28

Praying in the thick of it

Prepare

How do you feel when people treat you badly?
What do you do when you are treated badly?

Read   Psalm 28

Explore

The LORD is my strength and my shield; my heart trusts in him, and he helps me. My heart leaps for joy, and with my song I praise him.

Psalm 28:7 (NIV)

Psalm 28 is written by David in the midst of great difficulty and strife. He is surrounded by evildoers and confronted by hypocrites (v 3b). On every side he feels hemmed in by those who disregard God (v 5). It is a testing situation. He fears he might not even get through it, and knows that he needs God's help (v 1). So he calls out to the Lord his rock, desperate for help. David longs for justice (vs 4,5) – for the wicked to be punished (v 4) and that he will be treated differently (v 3).

The great turning-point comes in verse 6 where David receives his answer and the mercy for which he pleaded. Look at verse 7 where he applies this truth to his own heart, and in verses 8 and 9 he extends these truths to the rest of his people.

This is a great model for us in the midst of trying situations. Like David, let's turn our fears into prayers for the help, justice and mercy of God. He is our rock, our shield, our shepherd, our saving refuge, and the strengthener of his people. May it be our God in whom our heart trusts and worships, even in tough times.

Respond

Look back over all the images David uses to describe his God in Psalm 28. How does each one help you respond rightly to difficult situations, now or in the future?

Monday
26 November

2 Timothy 4:1–8

Preach the Word

> *Preach the word; be prepared in season and out of season; correct, rebuke and encourage – with great patience and careful instruction.*
>
> 2 Timothy 4:2 (NIV)

Prepare

What do you do when the truth of God's Word cuts across your life? Do you ignore it, alter it or align your life according to it? How do you feel about the person who tells you these truths from God's Word?

Read 2 Timothy 4:1–8

Explore

Paul charges Timothy to 'preach the word' (v 2), a simple command but with the enormous weight of verse 1 behind it, there is nothing that compares with its urgency.

Timothy is to preach when it is popular (in season) and when it is not (out of season). Timothy is to preach the Word in a way that it grows God's people in a healthy direction, which will require great patience and care. Not only will it be tough, it will also be opposed. People will seek to replace Timothy and his clear teaching with a chorus of alternatives who will tell them exactly what they want to hear (v 3).

This isn't the promise of a quiet and comfortable life, but one of hardship requiring careful balance (v 5) – a task made all the more important because Paul is soon to die (vs 6–8). So it will be left to Timothy to carry on this most vital task of preaching God's Word in a way that grows God's people.

Respond

'Father God, thank you for the gift of faithful preachers whose greatest desire is to preach your Word in a way that grows your people. Help them keep their heads in all situations. Help me to hear your words to me as they speak, and may your Word do your work in my life.'

2 Timothy 4:9–22

Safely home at last

Prepare

What does successful gospel ministry entail? Who is involved? What is needed?

Read

2 Timothy 4:9–22

Explore

As Paul prepares to sign off this final letter, he reflects on the people he has encountered. It is a very mixed bunch indeed.

Some started well but fell away, like Demas (v 10). Some have been dispatched on other duties, like Titus and Tychicus. Some have remained with him right up until the end, like Luke (v 11); whereas some who had parted company with Paul (see Acts 16) are now valuable for his ministry, like Mark (v 11). There is also a dearly loved group with Timothy in Ephesus whom Paul wants to encourage and make special mention of (vs 19,20).

Gospel work has always been team work, and Paul has invested himself in forging strategic partnerships for the flourishing of the gospel wherever he could. But there's opposition too – look at Paul's blunt warning in verses 14 and 15 about an individual who'll make ministry difficult for Timothy.

Notice Paul's attitude when facing the end of his life (vs 17,18) – not depressed and despondent, but trusting and triumphant. Paul is confident that God will protect him from each and every attack right up until the moment he calls him home.

> *The Lord will rescue me from every evil attack and will bring me safely to his heavenly kingdom. To him be glory for ever and ever. Amen.*
> 2 Timothy 4:18 (NIV)

Respond

If gospel work is team work, who can you partner with, invest in, encourage along? Pray for them now. How can you grow your relationship with them going forward?

Wednesday
28 November

Go for godliness

Paul, a servant of God and an apostle of Jesus Christ to further the faith of God's elect and their knowledge of the truth that leads to godliness ...

Titus 1:1 (NIV)

Prepare

What does godly living look like? What helps us to live godly lives? Think of some people you know who exemplify what godly living looks like.

Read   Titus 1:1–4

Explore

Paul is writing this letter to Titus, one of the next generation of young leaders who is serving on the island of Crete. The church is very young and Titus has a hard job on his hands strengthening and stabilising this fledgling congregation.

Right at the outset Paul points Titus to what is going to be the main theme of his letter: right knowledge of God leads to godly living. Look at verse 1 where Paul describes his ministry. Paul says plainly that growing people's knowledge of the gospel will grow them in godliness; that is, right thinking leads to right living. And right living is worthwhile because eternal life is on offer (v 2).

It is interesting today how technique-driven the world is. Ten steps to do this, three tips for doing that. Paul wants none of it. His model of ministry is that if you want people to live godly lives, the way to do that is to keep furthering their knowledge of God and his gospel.

Respond

If godly living is the fruit of godly thinking, how can you be growing in this direction? 'Father God, help me grow in godliness as I learn more about you. Help me gain a deeper understanding of who you are so that every area of my life might be lived in loving obedience to you.'

Titus 1:5–16

Sound doctrine

Prepare

Why should church leaders be sound in what they believe and consistent in how they live? What advantages does this bring to the congregation?

Read   Titus 1:5–16

Explore

Titus' key job on Crete was to appoint elders in every town (v 5) – to set in place leadership that will bring flourishing to the churches as they are led by godly men. In verses 6 to 9, Paul gives him a detailed list of characteristics to look for in those leaders. Try to summarise the big themes detailed in the list.

The overarching role of these leaders is detailed at the end of verse 9; they are to encourage people with sound doctrine, they are to teach them what is right and true. But they are also to refute what is false. They are to be shepherds who feed and lead their sheep in what is good, but also protect them from what is bad.

The following section adds weight to this role. It is an essential job because the Cretan church and Cretan society is fraught with danger. There are rebellious people teaching what is false (vs 10,14,16), and the society in Crete is full of ungodliness (vs 12,13). Without godly leaders this fledgling church will not survive.

The remedy to this precarious situation is godly leaders who will lead the church in godliness.

> *To the pure, all things are pure, but to those who are corrupted and do not believe, nothing is pure. In fact, both their minds and consciences are corrupted.*
>
> **Titus 1:15 (NIV)**

Respond

'Father God, help all my church leaders to live godly lives and hold firmly to the trustworthy message of the gospel. Help them encourage us in sound doctrine and give them courage and wisdom to refute what is wrong.'

Friday
30 November

Walking
adverts

In everything set them an example by doing what is good. In your teaching show integrity, seriousness and soundness of speech ...
Titus 2:7,8a (NIV)

Prepare

What difference does the gospel make to the way you live? How does the way you live contrast with others around you?

Read   Titus 2:1–15

Explore

Paul now takes Titus on a guided tour of different groups in his congregation and shows him what difference sound doctrine makes to the way they conduct themselves. The Christians on Crete are meant to be walking adverts for the power of the gospel. Paul tells Titus that in every way they must make the teaching about God our Saviour attractive (v 10). The Christians on Crete are to adorn the gospel. As people look at your life and the difference Jesus is making in it, would they be attracted to Jesus?

The gospel impacts every area of Cretan society from the older women to the young men, from the relationship between husbands and wives to the relationship between slaves and their masters. The sound doctrine of the gospel leads to sound living in the people. Titus himself is to set an example for the believers (v 7), giving his people a model of what the life of faith looks like and how the gospel transforms us.

Godly living doesn't come about by human effort (see vs 11–15). It is only by miraculous transformation through the power of the gospel. God is committed to his purpose of redeeming a people to love us as his very own, eager to do good (v 14).

Respond

Consider your life and the areas where godliness is lacking. Spend some time thinking about how the gospel should transform these attitudes, actions and behaviours. Then pray.

Bible in a Year
Hosea 1,2; Jude

Totally transformed

Prepare

Think about your life before you came to know Jesus. How is life different now? What were your attitudes and actions like before? What are they like now?

Read   Titus 3:1–15

Explore

In this final chapter of Titus, Paul takes time to remind the Cretans of their life before they met Jesus. He uses very unflattering language to describe their previous lives: foolish, disobedient, deceived, enslaved. He then reminds them – in some famous verses – of God's miraculous intervention. Take time to read verses 4 to 7 through slowly and even map it out with pen and paper. It is a wonderful summation of the gospel.

In the past the Cretans were foolish and disobedient. But then, through the gospel of grace, they were washed and renewed, brought into relationship with God, and given the hope of eternal life. This is not just their story, it is also our story – and it is a glorious story!

However, note that this is not a call to sit back, relax and chill until eternal life arrives – not at all. The Christians in Crete (and we) are to be devoted, passionate and wholehearted about doing what is good (v 8). All out and all in for doing what is right.

Paul then gives some examples of the negative – what devotion to doing good doesn't look like (vs 9–11).

… he saved us, not because of righteous things we had done, but because of his mercy. He saved us through the washing of rebirth and renewal by the Holy Spirit …
Titus 3:5 (NIV)

Respond

What would sheer devotion to doing what is good look like for you today? What things will you be engaged in? What things will you not? Pray and ask for God's help that you do it.

Sunday
2 December

The Lord is glorious

The LORD gives strength to his people; the LORD blesses his people with peace.

Psalm 29:11 (NIV)

Prepare

Think about the most powerful things you have seen in nature. How did you feel as you witnessed these events?

Read · Psalm 29

Explore

Eighteen times the name 'LORD' is repeated in this psalm. David is proclaiming the majesty and might of the Lord of heaven and earth.

He does this by giving us snapshots of God's impact on his creation. We start in the heavenly realms where angelic beings are commanded to ascribe glory to the Lord (vs 1,2). Then we move to the storm and the power the Lord has over it (vs 3,4). Next is the forest and how with simply his voice the Lord shatters the great cedars (v 5). He is sovereign over nations (v 6) and over nature (vs 7,8). God brings forth life but also lays it bare (v 9).

The only rightful response when faced with a God like this is to join the chorus of the 'all' at the end of verse 9 and declare, 'Glory!'

The clouds separate, revealing the Lord enthroned as the sovereign eternal ruler over all things (v 10). Yet he is not just a powerful God 'up there', but a personal God to his people, giving them strength and peace (v 11).

Respond

'Father God, thank you that you are Lord of all. A God of sovereign power and awesome might. Help me lean on you for strength and know your peace in my life. Help me cry 'Glory!' when I contemplate how good and how great you are.'

Bible in a Year
Hosea 7,8; Psalms 137,138

Spotlight on...
the hyssop

Like intricately woven threads, there are many themes that run through the Bible. One of them is found in this poignant passage in John's Gospel:

'Later, knowing that everything had now been finished, and so that Scripture would be fulfilled, Jesus said, "I am thirsty." A jar of wine vinegar was there, so they soaked a sponge in it, put the sponge on a stalk of the hyssop plant, and lifted it to Jesus' lips. When he had received the drink, Jesus said, "It is finished." With that, he bowed his head and gave up his spirit' (John 19:28–30).

This is the one who had said, 'Let anyone who is thirsty come to me and drink' (John 7:37); but now he is thirsty. This is the one who promised his disciples that a time was coming when they would drink the fruit of the vine together in his Father's kingdom (Matthew 26:29); but now he drinks bitter wine from the hand of

executioners. This is the one who said that he had come to bring life in all its fullness (John 10:10); but now, he dies. And yet, this is not defeat – 'It is finished'; that is, in this moment the Scriptures have been fulfilled and all he set out to achieve has been completed.

In these verses, John gives us a surprising detail – one of these intricately woven threads that run through Scripture – that illuminates the meaning of all of this. Did you notice we're told the type of bush that provided the stick used to lift the sponge to Jesus' lips? A hyssop branch. Why the horticultural detail?!

This particular plant actually features quite a bit in the Bible. Back in the ceremonial laws God gave to his people in Leviticus, hyssop was to be used for cleansing people and houses. For example, to cleanse a person after a skin disease, God tells the priests to use cedar wood, scarlet yarn, the blood of a bird, and hyssop (Leviticus 14:1–7). The same method was used to purify a house that previously had contained mould (Leviticus 14:33–53). So hyssop is associated with cleansing.

Again, hyssop is mentioned by King David in Psalm 51 – his song of repentance after committing adultery with Bathsheba (see 2 Samuel 11,12): 'Cleanse me with hyssop, and I shall be clean; wash me, and I shall be whiter than snow' (v 7). So David associates hyssop with cleansing from sin and averting God's judgement.

But hyssop also features in one of the most important events in the Bible. During the Passover, the Israelites were commanded to mark their doorposts with a lamb's blood so that the angel of death would pass over them and spare their firstborn sons (see Exodus 12). What did God tell them to use to paint the blood onto their doorposts (v 22)? A bunch of hyssop. The blood of the lambs was a sign that a substitute had died in the place of Israel's firstborn sons. To paint the doorposts with blood was an act of faith in God's deliverance. The hyssop signified that this faith made God's people clean in his sight.

This is why John tells us it was a hyssop branch the soldiers used to lift the bitter wine to Jesus' lips. It is in this moment that the cleansing of God's people is complete. The true 'Lamb of God' (see John 1:29) has shed his blood to cleanse his people from their sin. He dies in our place; he thirsts so that we can be satisfied; he tastes the bitterness of his Father's wrath at sin, so that one day we can enjoy sweet wine in the new creation with him for ever. It is finished, and we are clean.

Angus Moyes

Worship matters

Writer

John Grayston

Until 2009 John was the Director of Theology for Scripture Union England and Wales. Now retired but acting as Biblical and Theological Consultant for SU, and engaged in writing and itinerant preaching and teaching. John is a member of the leadership team at Tile Kiln Church in Chelmsford, he has three adult children and seven grandchildren.

Much of Chronicles repeats material from Samuel and Kings but with a different angle. It was written after the Exile to help those who had returned learn from their history. The writer has a special interest in the Temple and its worship, encouraging his readers to keep God at the centre. He focuses on the kings of Judah where the lesson is: obey God and things will go well, disobey him and they won't.

Our readings cover the period from Solomon (about 970 BC) to the return from exile (538 BC). From the glory of the Temple things go downhill. The kingdom splits, after which the writer is really only interested in the southern kingdom of Judah. There are bad and good kings, times of deserting God and times of restoration. All the time God is calling to his people, a call that often goes unheeded.

For much of the period the dominant powers are Assyria and Egypt, with Judah caught in the middle. At the start, Assyria is the top nation and eventually gains control over Judah before weakening and allowing Egypt to take brief control. Meanwhile Babylon is on the rise, defeats Egypt and a little later takes much of Judah into exile. This, says the writer, is the result of their sin.

Expect to gain a big vision of God – glorious and powerful, holy and just, patient and loving. Look out for the importance of keeping God at the centre of our worship and our daily lives.

Choose wisely – choose wisdom

Prepare

If there was one thing you could ask God for, what would it be? Why?

Read   2 Chronicles 1:1–17

Explore

1 Kings fills in extra background. Solomon did establish himself as king (v 1) but it wasn't without a struggle. What was the decisive factor (v 1)?

God is at the heart of the story. Solomon wants to ensure that worship is done properly but despite his eagerness he doesn't run ahead – he asks God for the best way. And then when God asks what he wants, the answer is wisdom to rule, to be a good king, to govern well. He knows he can't do that on his own; he needs God to show the way.

We are not called to be kings of Israel, but we are called to live effectively for God, to show Jesus to others. And we can't do that on our own. We need to know the right things to do, the sensitive things to say. And that is when, like Solomon, we ask God for wisdom. We don't ask for our own sake, we ask so that others may benefit (v 10). Whatever roles God has called us to we can be sure that if we ask he will give us what we need – and because he loves to give we may get more than we asked for (v 12).

> *'Give me wisdom and knowledge, that I may lead this people, for who is able to govern this great people of yours?'*
> 2 Chronicles 1:10 (NIV)

Respond

James encourages us to ask God for wisdom (James 1:5). Where do you need wisdom this week? Tough decisions? Awkward situations? Tricky relationships? Ask him for wisdom now.

Tuesday
4 December

Only the best

'The temple I am going to build will be great, because our God is greater than all other gods.'

2 Chronicles 2:5 (NIV)

Prepare

What will you do for God this week? How will you set about it?

Read   2 Chronicles 2:1–18

Explore

David's desire to build a temple was understandable and good. He wanted God to have his rightful place in national life. He was not the right man but passed his vision on to Solomon. Solomon realised that God couldn't be confined in a building (v 6), but he knew that it was an important way of focusing their worship. Sometimes we need things, places or people to help us meet with God. What are yours?

Only the best would do – materials, craftsmen, design, all combining to create a building that would honour God. It's a frequent theme in the Bible. Sacrifices, for example, had to be perfect (eg Leviticus 1:3) and the Israelites got into trouble when they palmed God off with second best (Malachi 1:7,8). How do we match up? Money, time, skills, abilities – does God get the first and the best?

It's not only Israel involved. Hiram king of neighbouring Tyre supplies materials and a highly skilled craftsman. Despite the polite language of Eastern negotiation, he does not worship the Lord. And yet he has a part to play. How can we involve in our activities people who don't yet follow Jesus? God's plans may be bigger than ours.

Respond

Review the activities you will be involved in for the rest of the week – at church, at work, in the home. Pray that God will help you do each one in ways that show him to others.

82

Bible in a Year
Hosea 11,12; Revelation 3

2 Chronicles 5:1–14

The heart of worship

Prepare

Think of some of the ways that God has shown his love to you. Thank him.

Read   2 Chronicles 5:1–14

Explore

Right at the heart of the Temple is the Ark of the Covenant, just as it had been in the Tabernacle. This box, covered in gold with two gold cherubim on top (Exodus 25:10–22), was the symbol of God's presence at the centre of their worship and national life, a constant reminder of his covenant with them. This covenant, or agreement, goes back to Exodus 19:1–6 where God promises to care for his people and they promise to live as he requires. Hence the tablets with the Ten Commandments. The Ark was a constant reminder of God's loving commitment and Israel's obligation to honour God in the way they lived.

As Christians we have a new covenant (Luke 22:20), based on the death of Jesus who revealed God's glory (vs 13,14) in an even greater way (John 1:14). Our relationship with God is guaranteed not on the basis of keeping a set of rules but on the basis of what Jesus has done for us. But that doesn't mean we can do as we like – he still expects us to live in ways that he wants and that show how much we love and respect him.

> *The priests then brought the ark of the LORD's covenant to its place in the inner sanctuary of the temple, the Most Holy Place, and put it beneath the wings of the cherubim.*
>
> 2 Chronicles 5:7 (NIV)

Respond

Thank God for his glory shown to you in Jesus; renew your commitment to please him in all you do and ask for the help of his Spirit.

Thursday
6 December

2 Chronicles 6:1–11

Worship
matters

'Praise be to the LORD, the God of Israel, who with his hands has fulfilled what he promised with his mouth to my father David.'

2 Chronicles 6:4 (NIV)

Prepare

Recall a time someone broke a promise to you. How did you feel?

Read   2 Chronicles 6:1–11

Explore

The Temple is the fulfilment of the promise to David. But there's more to it. God had told Moses that when the people arrived in the land he would choose a place where he would be worshipped (Deuteronomy 12). Solomon picks this up in verse 5, reminding Israel of God's faithfulness to his promises. Having a central place doesn't mean, as Solomon sees so clearly, that God was located in one place. It was a way of giving a godly focus to national life and preventing all sorts of strange worship practices springing up all over the place – which is what actually happened. Worship of a holy God is a serious matter – but it's also, as we have seen (5:13), an opportunity for joyful celebration.

God desires the worship of his people. He lays out how it should happen. It is to be focused on him and whenever it focuses on the things we like or on making us feel good we have lost sight of the most important thing. Patterns have changed over the years. We don't have a physical temple. But all that we do when we come together is about God, helping us to focus on him and equipping us to live for him.

Respond

Think about your own attitude to worship. What more could you do to ensure that you are completely focused on God?

2 Chronicles 6:12–42

Meeting point

Prepare

What do you find hardest about prayer? As you read, see if Solomon's prayer offers any way forward.

Read   2 Chronicles 6:12–42

Explore

This great prayer of dedication returns to some old themes: God's faithfulness, his power and majesty, the inability of buildings to contain him. But the central theme is that the Temple will be a meeting place. Here God will hear the prayers of his people and will respond in grace, mercy and forgiveness. He will bring justice (v 23). He will show them how to live (v 27). The Temple is a place of reconciliation where relationship with God is restored. They will sin and face God's judgement. When they come back to him, God will forgive. This isn't just for Israel; who else is involved (vs 32,33)? One of the things that upset Jesus was that Gentiles were not able to pray in the Temple (Mark 11:17). All nationalities can come freely to God.

When Solomon refers to God's 'anointed one' (v 42), he is thinking of himself. But we can see a bigger plan; that one day another descendant of David would come, that one greater than Solomon has come (Matthew 12:42) to open a new way to God. In him there is no condemnation (Romans 8:1), and when we do sin we know that we can be forgiven (1 John 1:9). We can be even more confident than Solomon, because we stand the other side of the cross.

> 'Hear the supplications of your servant and of your people Israel when they pray toward this place. Hear from heaven, your dwelling place; and when you hear, forgive.'
> 2 Chronicles 6:21 (NIV)

Respond

Pick one idea from this prayer and make it your own today, coming to God through Jesus.

Bible in a Year
Joel 3; Revelation 5

85

2 Chronicles 7:1–22

Glory!

When all the Israelites saw the fire coming down and the glory of the LORD above the temple, they knelt on the pavement with their faces to the ground, and they worshipped and gave thanks to the LORD, saying, 'He is good; his love endures for ever.'

2 Chronicles 7:3 (NIV)

Prepare

Sit quietly and focus on God. Ask him to show you more of himself.

Read   2 Chronicles 7:1–22

Explore

God comes in glory – again (5:13,14). How do we understand God's glory? It's not an easy idea to get hold of. It suggests worth, value, status. Here it refers to God's presence seen and felt by his people. What did they experience? Perhaps something like the pillars of cloud and fire in Exodus or the cloud at Sinai (see Exodus 24:17). Whatever actually took place, it was something both beautiful and awesome, attractive but overwhelming. Some of us will have had experiences of God a little like that when we feel very close to him.

How do we respond to such experiences of God? We recognise who God is – they lay face down on the ground (v 3). This is not a 'best mate' sort of God. He is the awesome and powerful creator of the universe. But he is also the One whose love endures for ever (vs 3,6). They worshipped in style, at some cost (v 5) and with enthusiasm (vs 6,8,10). Capturing this full vision of God is not easy. Somehow we have to hold together his power and majesty, his holiness and justice, his love and grace. When we meet together let's encourage one another to look for a bigger vision of God; let's never assume that we have discovered all there is.

Respond

Sit quietly again and focus on God. Let him remind you of all that he is. Praise him.

Bible in a Year
Amos 1,2; Revelation 6

Psalm 30

Complete turnaround

Sunday
9 December

Prepare

Think again of the God we saw in yesterday's reading. Powerful and glorious, loving and patient, present with his people. Thank him that he is with you now.

You turned my wailing into dancing; you removed my sackcloth and clothed me with joy.
Psalm 30:11 (NIV)

Read   Psalm 30

Explore

The heading to the psalm credits David as the author and indicates that it was used at the dedication of the Temple (although the Hebrew simply says the house). But it would certainly have been a fitting song to sing at the dedication. It celebrates God's deliverance. David had been in trouble of some sort (v 1), in which he called to God for help (vs 2,8,10). There is a hint in verse 5 that this was the result of some failure on his part. Look at verses 1 to 3 to see how he felt.

That is not the end of the story. God is in the transformation business. Judgement flows from God's holy character but he delights to show favour and love; these are the things that last (v 5).

In the tough times – whether we feel that they are the consequence of our sin and failure, or whether they are just stuff that happens – we have a choice. We can complain and be dragged down, or we can come to God believing that he can turn things around. Look back over the psalm. What do you see that encourages you to trust God?

Respond

What do you long for God to change? Pray about it now, encouraged by this psalm to believe that he can and will act.

Bible in a Year
Amos 3,4; Psalms 140,141

87

2 Chronicles 24:1–16

Giving and serving

All the officials and all the people brought their contributions gladly, dropping them into the chest until it was full.

2 Chronicles 24:10 (NIV)

Prepare

Thank God for the privilege of working with him. Ask him to show you how you might be more effective.

Read   2 Chronicles 24:1–16

Explore

We jump forward 17 chapters, about a hundred years, five kings and one queen. It's not been a good period. Under Solomon's son Rehoboam the kingdom has split into two. The kings in the southern part, Judah, have been a mixed bag. Queen Athaliah (v 7), heavily into Baal worship and a bloodthirsty tyrant, wiped out the rest of the royal family. With one exception; Joash has been hidden in the Temple, saved by the priest Jehoiada and his wife.

With Baal, one of the Canaanite gods, in favour, the Temple had been neglected. When we make other things our main interest our relationship with God always suffers. Joash sets out on a repair mission. But first a bit of fundraising, bringing back the tax which Moses introduced (Exodus 30:11–16). We fund our activities rather differently (and it will vary from one church group to another), but take a look at what happened here. They gave gladly and generously (check out 2 Corinthians 9:7) – there was even some left over. So, what about our giving? Glad? Generous? The workers worked hard (v 13, GNB). We've seen that before. And if we look into the New Testament we see it in people like Paul (1 Corinthians 15:10). That's a challenge for us in our service for God, but remember we have God working with us.

Respond

In prayer, review your approach to giving and serving. Is it generous? Is it glad?

Here we go again

Prepare

Ask God to show you how much he values you and how much he wants to do for you.

Read

2 Chronicles 29:1–11,35b,36

Explore

We move forward another hundred years or so. After the death of his godly mentor Jehoiada, Joash went off the rails and idolatry made a comeback (2 Chronicles 24:17–19). Meanwhile, the northern kingdom of Israel (of which the chronicler says very little) has been conquered by Assyria, and the people scattered.

So again the Temple is in disrepair and the worship of God in disarray. This is becoming a familiar story. It should not surprise us. It's a recurring pattern in the life of the nation. And we know from our own experience how easy it is to turn away from God and to allow other things to take over. It's often subtle and slow – we may not even spot it happening. We may try to justify it – it's not so important, God wants me to have a life, it doesn't take much time. There are consequences. Yet God always loves us and wants us back. He will try to get our attention although his methods may be less drastic than those used here (vs 8,9).

What we can be sure of is that when we turn back and give God his rightful place, he will not only welcome us but will do good things for us (v 36).

> *Hezekiah and all the people rejoiced at what God had brought about for his people, because it was done so quickly.*
>
> 2 Chronicles 29:36 (NIV)

Respond

Are there things in your life that are getting a little too much attention and taking God's place? Acknowledge your failure and ask God to help you sort it.

Wednesday
12 December

Come on
and celebrate

'If you return to the LORD, then your fellow Israelites and your children will be shown compassion by their captors and will return to this land, for the Lord your God is gracious and compassionate. He will not turn his face from you if you return to him.'

2 Chronicles 30:9 (NIV)

Prepare

Prepare by confessing any sin or failure that you are aware of, and ask God's forgiveness.

Read   2 Chronicles 30:1 – 31:1

Explore

Not only had the Temple been neglected; so had the central celebration of Jewish faith, the Passover. God's people were in danger of losing sight of what made them into a nation – God's deliverance from Egypt. The northern tribes are invited despite the division and scattering. As we so often find in our own experience, many when invited to meet with God show no interest (v 10), but others welcome the opportunity (vs 11,25). Divisions disappear when we make God the centre of our life and worship. Paul encouraged the church in Corinth to find unity in Communion, the Christian equivalent of the Passover (1 Corinthians 11:17–34).

It all happened in a bit of a hurry – many had not gone through the purifying process (v 17). Hezekiah's prayer brings God's forgiveness. Our heart attitude is more important than the letter of the law, a truth that Jesus underlined centuries later (Mark 7:1–11).

As they remembered all the good things God had done, they found forgiveness and healing (v 20). This Passover celebration stands in a line that stretches from Moses to Jesus. For Christian readers there is the encouragement to remember what God has done for us in Jesus and to find healing and forgiveness. We who have experienced God's salvation will want to be wholehearted and totally committed (31:1).

Respond

As we approach Christmas, thank God for what he has done for us in Jesus.

90

Bible in a Year
Amos 9; Revelation 9

2 Chronicles 33:1–25

Thursday
13 December

Humility
wins

Prepare

Look back over some of your life with God. Think of all that he has done for you. Let it remind you that he alone is God.

Read   2 Chronicles 33:1–25

Explore

The familiar theme again. Hezekiah wasn't without fault (2 Chronicles 32:24–26). His son Manasseh is a bit of a puzzle. Much of his life was evil and idolatrous. As far as the writer of 2 Kings is concerned that's it. End of story. But here's another story, one of his captivity, repentance and restoration (vs 10–13). Both books are selective and had their own purpose, so perhaps they have chosen to tell different parts of the story.

As far as the Chronicler is concerned, Manasseh is a bad king who comes good. But not in his own strength. He responds to the wake-up call of his captivity, by repenting and turning to God. He humbled himself (v 12), a key theme in Chronicles (see 2 Chronicles 7:14). Pride leads us away from God; humility brings us back. Yesterday we met God's grace in his response to Hezekiah. Here it is again. That's God's nature – and looking back from this side of the death and resurrection of Jesus we have an even better opportunity to appreciate it. If there's hope for Manasseh, there's hope for anyone. But we mustn't cheapen God's grace. Remaining faithful, staying close to God and dealing with any sin or failure quickly are the ways to receive God's grace.

And when he prayed to him, the Lord was moved by his entreaty and listened to his plea; so he brought him back to Jerusalem and to his kingdom. Then Manasseh knew that the Lord is God.

2 Chronicles 33:13 (NIV)

Respond

Pray for those you know who need to respond to God's wake-up call, that they may turn to him.

Bible in a Year
Obadiah; Psalms 142,143

Friday
14 December

Back to the future

Prepare

Think about the way that the Bible has shaped your life. Ask God to speak to you again today through the power of his written Word.

Read   2 Chronicles 34:1–33

Explore

Familiar ground – again. True, but each of these renewals in the life of Judah has a new element. Joash restored the Temple, Hezekiah reinstated the Passover and now Josiah brings the law back to its rightful place. Each renewed the covenant, reminding people of God's commitment to them and calling them back to God. Josiah's reforms are centred on obedience to the law (v 31). But, as we shall see, these reforms don't go deep. Jeremiah, who was prophesying around this time, saw the superficiality of the response and, inspired by God, looked forward to a new covenant, which would change not just the outward, but the deep inner motivation (Jeremiah 31:31–34).

Temple, worship, law and covenant shaped Israel's relationship with God. Jesus (John 2:21) and the church (Ephesians 2:21) take on the role of the Temple, Passover gives way to Communion as a reminder of salvation through Jesus. The law functions in a different way, but still helps us understand what God expects of us as his people. Jesus' death introduces the new covenant of which Jeremiah spoke (Matthew 26:27–29). We have so much more, giving us an even greater motivation to live as God wants.

Respond

As Christians, our lives are shaped by this new understanding of temple, worship, law and covenant. How does that show in our lives?

Bible in a Year
Jonah 1,2; Revelation 10

2 Chronicles 36:2–23

Saturday
15 December

Disaster – or not?

Prepare

Try to put yourself in the place of God as he sees the repeated failure of his people. How do you think he feels?

Read   2 Chronicles 36:2–23

Explore

The story is coming to its tragic end – except that is not the end. Josiah met his death at the hands of Pharaoh Necho (the king of Egypt in verse 4), then the Babylonians took over and things in Judah spiralled out of control until the fall of Jerusalem in 587/6 BC.

Both Kings and Chronicles see this as a direct consequence of Judah's rebellion and idolatry. They brought it on themselves. This was not what God had wanted – so many messengers (24:19) and such little result (v 15; see too Matthew 21:33–46). God still patiently, lovingly reaches out to those who have turned their backs on him. There is always a way back for prodigals if only they will take it (Luke 15:11–32). Judgement is always something that we bring on ourselves (John 3:18). Verse 21 underlines this; the land itself was affected and needed time to recover. Human sin has far-reaching effects.

As things collapsed, the prophets (at this point, Jeremiah, as we saw yesterday) pointed to a new hope. The return from exile was a further mark of God's grace (v 23). But the final and greatest act of grace was yet to be.

> *The LORD, the God of their ancestors, sent word to them through his messengers again and again, because he had pity on his people and on his dwelling-place.*
>
> 2 Chronicles 36:15 (NIV)

Respond

Pray for any you know who have turned away from God, asking that they might come to their senses (Luke 15:17).

Bible in a Year
Jonah 3,4; Revelation 11

93

Sunday
16 December

Hang in there

> But I trust in you,
> Lᴏʀᴅ; I say, 'You are my
> God.' My times are in
> your hands.
>
> Psalm 31:14,15 (NIV)

Prepare

As you look around, what causes you pain? What do you find puzzling or disturbing?

Read — Psalm 31

Explore

According to the heading, David wrote this psalm, but it fits well with the struggles we have just been reading about. Jeremiah echoes the words of verse 13 (Jeremiah 6:25; 20:3). Israel was clinging to worthless idols (v 6). There were those who trusted in God (v 14), but as here the overall story was one of godlessness.

So how does this psalm speak into our situations? Like David and like Jeremiah, we feel the pressure and pain of living among those who have no time for God, who chase the idols of money, status, sex or anything else that takes their fancy. The casual and ubiquitous, 'O my God' or in social media terms 'OMG', is a painful reminder that despite the words, few people take God seriously. How do we respond? We acknowledge the pain of living among those who have no time for God (v 6), trust God for our own protection (v 14), live in the hope that God will bring blessing (vs 19–21), encourage others to remain true to God (v 23) and tell our faith story as David did.

God will bring us through. But it may not be an easy road. Sometimes there seems no way forward (vs 10–14), and all we can do is hang on and leave it with God.

Respond

Ask God to keep you true to him. If you are finding it hard to trust him, ask for his strength.

Bible in a Year
Micah 1–3; Psalm 144

SHARING THE
GOOD NEWS WITH THE
NEXT GENERATION

Eight new booklets from Scripture Union
available in packs of ten for £5 each

BOOKLETS FOR 5–8s

THE BEST PRESENT EVER

THE BIGGEST SURPRISE

What do you believe?

WHO IS THE Light?

BOOKLETS FOR 8–11s

The GREATEST GIFT of all TIME

THE MOST MIND-BOGGING MYSTERY!

WHAT IS BEING A CHRISTIAN ALL ABOUT?

DO YOU WANT DARKNESS COMES TO VISIT?

True story

Writer

Jo Swinney

Jo Swinney is Director of Church Communications at CPO, a speaker and an author, most recently of Home: the quest to belong *(Hodder & Stoughton). She has an MA in Theology from Regent College, Vancouver, and lives in Surbiton with her husband and their two daughters.*

We live in strange times, times when public figures lie boldly, repeatedly and seemingly without repercussion; times when tolerance of difference is valued more highly than logic, which dictates competing claims cannot all be right; times when individual freedom to choose what to believe has led to mass confusion.

Luke's 'orderly account' (1:3) of the time around the birth of Jesus and his early life is written for his friend Theophilus, 'that [he] might know the certainty of the things [he] has been taught.' He gives specific details – times, places and names. He progresses through the events chronologically, presenting them without hyperbole or interpretation. He lays out the fruit of his careful investigation and here it is for us to read, all these years later.

Whatever the spirit of this age might say, truth is not a matter of opinion. Jesus said he was 'the way, the truth and the life' – that no one could come to the Father except through him (John 14:6). The stories of his birth and early life add to the picture of this man who claimed to be God. They add to the credibility of the idea that he was who he said he was.

Faith demands a certain suspension of disbelief, a willingness not to lean on our own understanding. But we also have God-given minds, and orderly accounts for our minds to evaluate. Does Luke's reporting of these extraordinary events have the ring of truth? You decide.

A miracle baby

Prepare

'Sing to the LORD a new song, for he has done marvellous things' (Psalm 98:1).

Read   Luke 1:1–25

Explore

Luke's account begins with an angelic announcement, a miraculous pregnancy and a God-favoured, God-blessed, God-named baby boy. But Jesus is still in the wings. The story begins with John.

John's parents are an upright, devout couple named Zechariah and Elizabeth. They have served God faithfully, and yet they live with the sorrow and cultural shame of childlessness (v 25). One day, it is Zechariah's turn to burn incense in the Temple. He disappears inside, while the gathered worshippers pray and wait for him to emerge. And wait. And wait until it becomes concerning. They know full well God's holy presence can be dangerous.

Inside the Temple, Zechariah had been waylaid by an angel named Gabriel, and Gabriel had given him some news he was struggling to believe. After the death of all reasonable hope, he was to become a father.

Generations before, an elderly Sarah had laughed in the same set of circumstances (Genesis 18:12) and then became the matriarch of a nation. Zechariah's son would also have a significant role to play in God's world-saving plan. He would prepare the way for Jesus, the Messiah.

But the angel said to him: 'Do not be afraid, Zechariah; your prayer has been heard. Your wife Elizabeth will bear you a son, and you are to call him John.'

Luke 1:13 (NIV)

Respond

'Almighty God of miracles, forgive me for the times when I doubt you. Thank you for the miracle of baby John, sign of your favour to the whole of your creation. Amen.'

Tuesday
18 December

The angel and the virgin

> The angel answered, 'The Holy Spirit will come on you, and the power of the Most High will overshadow you. So the holy one to be born will be called the Son of God.'
>
> Luke 1:35 (NIV)

Prepare

God sent Gabriel to Zechariah and Mary to convey his message. How has he spoken to you? How ready are you to hear his voice and obey? Ask the Holy Spirit to soften your heart and sharpen your hearing.

Read   Luke 1:26–38

Explore

Both Zechariah and Mary responded to Gabriel with fear, and both questioned him about the logistics of what he foretold. But while Zechariah was struck dumb in retribution, Mary was given a gentle and clear answer. Her baby was to be God's child, conceived by the power of the Most High. And to reassure her of God's ability to do all things, Elizabeth's impossible pregnancy was well established.

I think there are several reasons for the different way Gabriel spoke to these two. Mary was young; Zechariah old enough to have learned to trust God. Mary had everything to lose – her future husband, her reputation, even her life; Zechariah had it all to gain. Mary's response was one of curiosity rather than disbelief; Zechariah wanted something more than Gabriel's word before he'd accept it.

What must it have been like to be told you had been chosen to give birth to a child who would rule over a never-ending kingdom? Mary's simple faith and obedience are quite extraordinary – an inspiration and a challenge to all of us who encounter her story.

Respond

'Lord I am your servant. Help me willingly submit to whatever you ask of me as Mary did. Amen.'

Bible in a Year
Micah 6,7; Revelation 13

Luke 1:39–45

Blessed

Prepare

Give thanks to God for the friends who build up your faith.

Read   Luke 1:39–45

Explore

Luke doesn't embellish or extrapolate in his 'orderly account'. He doesn't, for example, try to put across the fear Mary must have felt once this God-conceived baby began to make its presence known in her body. She knew she had not broken faith with Joseph, but she must have known also that her story was going to be a hard sell.

Mary's decision to head to the home of Elizabeth was a wise one. Elizabeth was primed and ready to welcome her with open arms and a Spirit-inspired reminder that Mary was blessed beyond all measure to be carrying this baby. Blessed, though this baby would put her future marriage at risk. Blessed, though this baby would mean years as a refugee in Egypt. Blessed, though she would one day watch him tortured and killed.

We speak of blessing lightly and often – after sneezes, in lieu of thanks, when the sun shines for our picnics. But God's blessing is of a different order. Elizabeth recognised God's blessing of Mary and declared it loudly and clearly. This was a gift more precious than the combined gifts from a million 'baby showers'.

> *'Blessed is she who has believed that the Lord would fulfil his promises to her!'*
>
> Luke 1:45 (NIV)

Respond

'Lord, if I am looking for signs of your blessing in the wrong places, forgive me. Thank you for blessing me beyond all measure with the gift of your Son, the presence of the Holy Spirit and the promise of a forever life with you. Thank you. Amen.'

Thursday
20 December

Luke 1:46–56

A vocabulary for prayer

And Mary said: 'My soul glorifies the Lord ...'
Luke 1:46 (NIV)

Prepare

'I will extol the LORD at all times; his praise will always be on my lips' (Psalm 34:1).

Read

Luke 1:46–56

Explore

The American pastor and author Eugene Peterson writes, 'Scripture without prayer has no soul; prayer without Scripture has no substance'.* One of the things that strikes me about Mary's joyful outburst here is how biblically resonant it is. She has a vocabulary for prayer garnered from ancient texts; texts she has clearly absorbed to the extent that when she opens her mouth to express extreme emotion, out comes the Bible.

The book of 1 Samuel begins with the story of Hannah. Hannah is childless and it is destroying her. Year after year she comes to the Temple to plead with God, and eventually she conceives and gives birth to a child, Samuel. Samuel's birth signifies a huge reversal of fortunes for Hannah, who was in a polygamous marriage as the only childless wife.

Her story and Mary's are different in many ways; but both women were humble, God-fearing and wide-eyed with wonder at God's intervention in their lives. And Hannah's words help Mary find expression for what is happening to her: 'My heart rejoices in the LORD. Those who were full hire themselves out for food, but those who were hungry are hungry no more. The LORD sends poverty and wealth; he humbles and he exalts. He raises the poor from the dust ... he seats them with princes' (from 1 Samuel 2:1–10).

Respond

Use Mary's song as a basis for your prayers today.

* *Kingfisher's Fire*, Hodder & Stoughton, 2017, p93

Bible in a Year
Habakkuk 1–3; Psalm 145

Godly gossip

Prepare

Take a moment to be still in the presence of God.

Read   Luke 1:57–66

Explore

Western 21st century societies place high value on independence and freedom; fewer and fewer people live close to extended family, and while we might share our news to our 'friends' on Facebook, most of us are not generally much impacted by our neighbours' lives.

Today's reading conveys how vastly different things were in first-century Palestine. Elizabeth's pregnancy was hot news and gave an emotional lift to the whole community (v 58). His name was a matter for neighbours and relatives (v 59), and Elizabeth and Zechariah's intervention and choice was highly unusual (v 63). Add to the mix Zechariah being struck dumb for almost a year and the child entering the world manifestly filled with the Spirit and you had a situation that captivated the entire community and beyond.

It might seem that Jesus arrived on the scene somewhat quietly, but these people from the nation through whom God had chosen to bless the entire world were buzzing with anticipation. From before he was even conceived, John was preparing the way. First his father, then his mother, his relatives, his neighbours and his countrymen could talk of nothing but what God was up to. This story is still intriguing, history-shaping, worthy of sharing. Are you helping it spread?

> *Everyone who heard this wondered about it, asking, 'What then is this child going to be?' For the Lord's hand was with him.*
>
> Luke 1:66 (NIV)

Respond

'Lord, fill me with excitement and the enthusiasm to talk to my family, friends and neighbours about the meaning of your birth this Christmas. Amen.'

Bible in a Year
Zephaniah 1–3; Revelation 15

Saturday
22 December

Sunrise

> He has raised up a
> horn of salvation for
> us in the house of his
> servant David (as he
> said through his holy
> prophets of long ago).
>
> Luke 1:69,70 (NIV)

Prepare

'Shine your light into the dark corners of my life, Lord. Thank you for your tender mercy. Amen.'

Read   Luke 1:67–80

Explore

This was an extraordinary time to be alive for the faithful of Israel. They had been waiting for salvation from the line of David for 14 generations (see the genealogy in Matthew 1). And filled with the Holy Spirit, Zechariah is able to pronounce the wait is over: the Lord 'has come to his people and redeemed them' (v 67). The night has been long, but day is dawning.

Luke's account is brilliantly constructed to capture both the granular, domestic details of the birth and life of Christ, and its cosmic significance. The detail provides the texture of a credible narrative; the sign-posting to significance alerts us to the gravity of the events as they unfold. John's birth is like the first rays of the sun brightening the sky. As his father predicted, he would go on to preach repentance and forgiveness, paving the way for Jesus' message. And as he prophesied, Jesus, whose radiance is able to dispel the shadow of death (v 79), through whom God's mercy shines (v 78), was God's fulfilment of his ancient covenant (v 72).

Respond

As we revisit very familiar stories over this Christmas season, let's pray for a divinely given alertness to the meaning of them. Let's pledge not to sleepwalk through this opportunity to be woken up to the 'rising' (v 78) of the Son of Man whose light penetrates the deepest darkness.

Luke 2:1–14

Sunday
23 December

World peace

Prepare

This can be a busy season and if we are not careful we can miss the opportunity to contemplate the mysterious and wonderful birth Christmas is all about. Lay down your lists, plans and concerns, and give Jesus your full attention.

Read   Luke 2:1–14

Explore

Caesar Augustus is considered to be the first Roman Emperor. He was the sole ruler of a vast and expanding empire and had almost unimaginable power. Under his leadership, the Roman Empire attained an unprecedented stability, known as the *Pax Romana*. Augustus was given credit for bringing worldwide peace and worshipped as 'Saviour' and 'Lord'. In a scruffy corner of Palestine, an unmarried mother-to-be and her fiancé made a journey from home at Caesar's bidding. He wanted to know who he had living under his control and so they went to be counted at the mandated location (vs 1–3).

And there he fades from the story and Jesus takes centre stage. Born in obscurity and laid in an animal feeding trough for want of anywhere better (v 7), this baby has had more influence over world events than Caesar Augustus could ever have dreamed of. As the angels told the shepherds, Jesus was – and is – the true Saviour (v 11). And Jesus would bring a peace far more profound than the absence of war. He would reconcile the whole of creation with its maker (Romans 8:20–25) and for humankind: the offer of salvation (v 14).

> *Today in the town of David a Saviour has been born to you; he is the Messiah, the Lord.*
> Luke 2:11 (NIV)

Respond

Thank God for the peace his favour brings.

Bible in a Year
Zechariah 1,2; Psalms 146,147

Monday
24 December

It all checks out

The shepherds returned, glorifying and praising God for all the things they had heard and seen, which were just as they had been told.

Luke 2:20 (NIV)

Prepare

'Taste and see that the LORD is good' (Psalm 34:8). Consider the tangible ways God has shown you his goodness.

Read

Luke 2:15–20

Explore

It was an ordinary night – the flocks quiet, the air still. And then: blazing light, a terrifying, glorious angelic figure addressing them, *them* – lowly shepherds – and the sky filling with more of these beings, making an unearthly sound that they could somehow understand, announcing the arrival of the Messiah in a town a stone's throw away. And then the inky darkness once more, the sheep settling down, silence ringing in their ears.

Before they could convince themselves they'd gone collectively mad, they set off to verify what they'd been told. Somewhere in Bethlehem, if this whole story was to be believed, there would be a newborn baby in a manger of all places. Sure enough, there he was. They saw him with their own eyes.

There is nothing abstract about God's interaction with his world. It is local, specific, concrete and very, very real. As the shepherds heard and then went to check it out, we are invited to experience a direct relationship with God too. And then pass on what we've found to be true to anyone who will listen.

Respond

'Lord, I am not satisfied with second-hand accounts of who you are. I want to know you. I want to experience your presence. Thank you that you are here with me now. Amen.'

The waiting game

Prepare

As Mary pondered over all that was said about Jesus in her heart, do the same on this day we celebrate and remember the birth of the Messiah. Mull over the details Luke has given us. Consider the impact Jesus has had on the world, and on you.

Read   Luke 2:21–35

Explore

Do you remember how the build-up to Christmas felt when you were a child? In my home, we started to get excited pretty early – around the time the clocks went back and we needed the heating on in the evenings. The closer the big day came, the more slowly the days seemed to pass. It was like a vaguely pleasant form of torture!

The people of Israel had been waiting for their Saviour for so long that many had given up thinking about him at all. It was just too hard to be expectant when they couldn't predict the time frame. But one man hadn't lost his focus. Simeon was 'righteous and devout' (v 25), and God rewarded him for his hopeful anticipation: before he died, he cradled the infant Jesus in his arms.

We live in the part of the story after one of the major hinges in the plot, but before the grand climax. We have some waiting to do ourselves, and we quite possibly won't see the finale, the coming of heaven to earth, in our lifetime. As the writer to the Hebrews urged, let's 'run with perseverance the race marked out for us, fixing our eyes on Jesus, the pioneer and perfecter of faith' (Hebrews 12:1,2).

Now there was a man in Jerusalem called Simeon, who was righteous and devout. He was waiting for the consolation of Israel, and the Holy Spirit was on him.

Luke 2:25 (NIV)

Respond

However you celebrate Christmas, make sure your eyes are fixed on Jesus, the one Simeon was waiting for, and the one whose return we still await today.

Bible in a Year
Zechariah 5,6; Revelation 18

Luke 2:36–40

When life gives you lemons

> *… she had lived with her husband seven years after her marriage, and then was a widow until she was eighty-four. She never left the temple but worshipped night and day, fasting and praying.*
>
> Luke 2:36,37 (NIV)

Prepare

'Lord, may the eyes of my heart be enlightened so I may know the hope to which you have called me, the riches of your glorious inheritance and your incomparably great power. Amen' (from Ephesians 1:18,19).

Read   Luke 2:36–40

Explore

Anna is one of those people in the Bible it would be easy to miss. She doesn't have a big or particularly dramatic role and if you were around at the time it might have been easy to write her off as a slightly batty and intense old lady. But even from the scanty details we have about her, there is enough to give us pause.

Seven short years into her marriage, Anna became a widow. Widows at that time were among the most vulnerable of society, to be pitied and feared for. This was not the life Anna would have chosen for herself. But look what she does with her remaining years: she moves into the Temple and devotes herself to worship and prayer. By the age of 84 Anna is so finely attuned to the voice of God she immediately recognises Jesus as the one who will redeem Jerusalem.

When things go wrong I often succumb to self-pity and 'if onlys'. Anna inspires me to remember that a life lived for God can always be made beautiful. I hope her story will be a gift to you today whatever you may be facing.

Respond

Pray that the Holy Spirit would show you the struggles you are facing in a new light.

Bible in a Year
Zechariah 7,8; Revelation 19